MW00464785

SEMIOTEXT(E) INTERVENTION SERIES

© Sayak Valencia, 2018.

Published by Semiotext(e)
PO BOX 629, South Pasadena, CA 91031
www.semiotexte.com

Translation Editing: Erica Mena

Design: Hedi El Kholti

ISBN: 978-1-63590-012-5
Distributed by The MIT Press, Cambridge, Mass.
and London, England
Printed in the United States of America

10 9 8 7 6 5 4 3 2

Sayak Valencia

─────────────────

Gore Capitalism

Translated by John Pluecker

semiotext(e)
intervention
series □ 24

Contents

To everyone who is engaged in daily rebellion
grounded in their own minority becoming.

Warning / *Advertencia*

In this book, our aim is not to develop a unitary, hegemonic feminism based on a simplistic critique of violence as foundational to the logics of gore capitalism. We are grounded in a multiplicity of feminisms and we posit the relevance of all of these both as geopolitically-situated systems of knowledge and as responses to specific contexts in which they developed. We believe that these feminisms must not be judged within the "impermeable" structures of white First World feminism. The feminism posited here departs from white First World feminism in its self-reflexiveness and rejects being closely linked to or used "by the imperialist cultural exploitation of feminism" (Chakrovorty, 1999, 303). We do not seek white discourses "nor white men looking to save brown women from brown men" (Chakrovorty, 1999, 303); we do not need First World discourses to explain the realities of the g-local Third World.[1]

On the contrary, we believe that First World[2] discourse should pay attention to what Third World discourses have to say about the evolution of the world of capital and of the world more generally. Reinterpretations of economic roles emerge precisely in the interstices of these peripheral worlds. In these spaces we have seen the creation of new identities and subjects in a broad spectrum ranging from the endriago subjects of gore capitalism to the creation of subjectivities that resist feeding into the static loop of white, heterosexual, masculinist formulas. These new resistant forms do not assume power to be equivalent to violence, but that rather upend that dyad to observe it from novel perspectives, which are able to produce and to imagine new methods for the use of the body, power and desire.

In this book, we argue against positioning oneself in a *benevolent hierarchy* that would stereotype the Third World as a precarious and vulnerable reality exclusively found in the global South; the vulnerability and precarity are real to a large extent, but only insofar as they are a result of the demands and requirements exported from the economic centers and major world powers and distributed by globalization through the media.

To conceive of the Third World as a geopolitically immutable space—without any possibility for action, empowerment, or the creation of its own discursive frame—is a clear indication of the disdain implicit in a colonialist position. This book does not posit a naïve, partial reading of our realities that—absolving ourselves of responsibility—might suggest the dystopias of globalization belong exclusively to the Third World; nor does it argue that the only possible contributions to globalization (from the other worlds) might be from the position of victims or executioners (or as distributors of organized crime around the globe.)

We do not want abstract discourses disconnected from the body, but instead discourses that are able to re-frame the causes, extent and persistence of violence in the gore-ridden Third World. We want discourses that refuse to appeal to victimization and the nullification of our subjectivities and agency. We want discourses that refuse to rely on reductionist and paternalist thinking that would deny the power of our concrete actions.

We do not seek saviors or discourses of salvation, but rather for our own process of empowerment to be recognized as subjects of the same order and with the same validity as Western subjects, yet without being categorized or translated as identical to them or as a monolith.

Thus, without neglecting our differences, we seek the creation of our own discourses that nurture a transfeminism that confronts and questions our contemporary situation, a situation that is invariably circumscribed by the logic of gore capitalism. By saying this, we do not mean for this book to reject, or fail to recognize, the theoretical and practical work of diverse forms of feminism and their existence throughout history. On the contrary, the fact that our discourse is careful not to dehistoricize the feminist movement—since in fact, we think it is crucial to know this history and to remember it—means that we recognize the important discursive contribution made by feminist movements to the construction of categories that both explain and locate us in relation to the world. In particular, we recognize the importance of the construction of a discursive corpus that has rendered us visible as a movement founded on network; this body of discourse has established the feminist condition as an epistemological category, and simultaneously preserved it as a condition of certain subjects (not exclusively ciswomen) and as a social movement.

For this reason, we join Judith Butler in saying: "It seems more crucial than ever to disengage feminism from its First World presumption and to use the resources of feminist theory and activism to rethink the meaning of the tie, the bond, the alliance, the relation, as they are imagined and lived in the horizon of a counter-imperialist egalitarianism."[3]

We seek an explanation of contemporary events that is not mistaken either for an acquittal or a moral indictment of the violence, nor delimited exclusively by moral judgment, in order to re-think the structuring role that violence plays in the evolution of capitalism and in its culmination as gore.

We seek, then, a transfeminism that would allow us to think beyond the limits of our current options. We believe that in any given context of oppression, we are forced to create theoretical and practical instruments that help us map out our strategies. We are clear that when there is only one option to choose from, we have to be capable of remaking that very option. To conclude then, if no other option is available, may that choice not be the end of us, but rather through our daily insur-rection may it come to re-signify us.

Esto es Tijuana

The fury of clouds that is the Pacific Ocean.

A dismembered torso strewn across the highway at rush hour. Cigarettes lit in rapid succession. The neon lights of the red-light district, microscopic universes. Arboreal metastasis.

Narcos. Machismo. Silicone Land. Whore-Barbie's Factory. High caliber weapons laughing, cackling. *Esto es Tijuana.*

Leaving and staying at the same time. Finding another way to say that everything is an eternal return. Irrevocable trajectories and irrevocable women. Violence, tedium and the everyday grind: overdrawn on all accounts. *Esto es Tijuana.*

The word *Bienvenidos* laughing in my face. The word *Bienvenidos* meaning every entrance is an exit. Silence stabs. The desert boils. Migrant screams ring out. *Esto es Tijuana.*

Donkey-zebras imitating nostalgia. Shiny new cars. Enraged taxis. The head repeats an atrocious mantra, "open (yourself) up on the inside." Get into the game. See the Fire. Escape constantly and once and for all bet on winning. *Esto es Tijuana.*

Where the questions where, when and why might not exist, the same as the word "never." Where half of the half does not compute. Where *Interminably* is the same as *Now.*

City of *over and over again.* Where the truth is never known. Where all words—including the word incest—portend multiple histories. Where *mi casa es su casa.* Where *su casa no es mi casa.* Where yes, actually, *su casa es mi caza*: I'm on a hunt and your house is my prey. *Esto es Tijuana.*

La línea never frees itself from the metallic serpent on either side.

A *frontera*-woman looks like death and walks with one hand on her revolver. The syringe-man unsuccessfully attempts to fly along the middle of the metal serpent. The transparent and the true. The piercing.

The first and the third world. The border. El bordo. Hell. The other part of the other side. The other side of the other side. The *This* side of the *Other* side. The happy world of disenchantment. *Esto es Tijuana.*

The limit. The perimeter. The edge of the world. He/she/they/what is dragged behind. The shore that licks white, middle-class, civilized culture and brings it to its end. The time bomb that detonates us. San Diego's garage.

The divided sea laughing raucously *entre las olas. Entre Las Solas.* In the waves and in all the women on their own. The grayness. The paradox. *Esto es Tijuana.*

The *copyright* of the end. *Cartel-right.* Gore capitalism. *Hotels, attractions, nightlife, restaurants, weather and border crossing…*

A blind search for combinatorics. Two million possibilities. *Crunchy, spicy and totally addictive-fabulous blends. Depictions of sodomy, bestiality, alternative sexual practices, racial and ethnic stereotypes. This is Tijuana.*

Everything that enters or leaves the city comes from two parts. Everything here leaves in two or more parts. *You can have whatever you can buy.* City of businesses. Virgin girls *for sale.* Affordable prices for foreigners. Luis Donaldo Colosio Acribillado (a.k.a Bullet-Riddled). Música de banda. Morgue. Techno. NAFTA. *Esto es Tijuana.*

La Tía Juana, Tiguana, Tiuana, Teguana, Tiwana, Tijuan, Ticuan, TJ, Tijuas: you can call her whatever you want because Tijuana—like every other word—means nothing and means: "beside the sea."

Esto es *Queerland.* "Aquí empieza la patria / The homeland begins here."

Esto es Tijuana.

At the brink of el bordo, I become blade.

Tijuana is affectionate. Unfathomable. Full of possibilities.

To be in love with a psychopath and to say so with a smile.

You should leave now. This is Tijuana.

Introduction

> Globalization is not a serious concept. We [US Americans] have invented it in order to disguise our policies of economic entry into other countries.
>
> —John Kenneth Galbraith

We propose the term *gore capitalism* to refer to the reinterpretation of the hegemonic global economy in (geographic) border spaces. As an example of this phenomenon, we propose the city of Tijuana, located at the border between Mexico and the United States and known as *the far corner of Latin America*.

We take the term "gore" from a genre of films characterized by extreme, brutal violence. Thus, "gore capitalism" refers to the undisguised and unjustified bloodshed that is the price the Third World pays for adhering to the increasingly demanding logic of capitalism. It also refers to the many instances of dismembering and disembowelment, often tied up with organized crime, gender and the predatory uses of bodies. In general, this term posits these incredibly brutal kinds of violence as tools of *necroempowerment*.[1]

Bodies are here conceived of as products of exchange that alter and break capital's logics of production, subverting the terms of capital by substituting commodity production with a commodity-made-flesh in the body and human life, through predatory techniques of extreme violence like kidnapping and contract murder.

Thus, when we say gore capitalism, we refer to the disruption of values and practices taking place (most visibly) in border territories, where one must ask "what converging types of strategies are being developed by subalterns—the marginalized—[...] under the transnationalizing forces of the First World" (hooks et al. 2004, 81).

Unfortunately, many of the *strategies* for confronting the First World are ultraviolent forms of capital accumulation,[2] practices that we categorize as gore. To further clarify this term: whereas in the first volume of *Capital* Marx writes that, "The wealth of societies in which the capitalist mode of production prevails appears as an immense accumulation of commodities" (Marx, 1992, 15), in gore capitalism this process is redirected and the destruction of the body becomes in itself the product or commodity; the only kind of accumulation possible now is through a body count, as death has become the most profitable business in existence.

We do not seek purity, correctness or incorrectness in the application of the logic of capitalism and its intended and unintended consequences. We do not seek to make value judgments, but rather to provide evidence of the failure of neoliberal discourse to explain said phenomena. Contemporary approaches are insufficient to theorize the gore practices that are now found around the world; this fact shows the need for such theorization in *a world in which there is no space outside capitalism's reach* (Jameson, 1992). Not conceptualizing gore practices does not do away with them, but merely renders them invisible or discusses them using language that creates a double standard inside of a theory, where terms like *black market* refer to economic practices *specific* to the Third World, since they are already considered *illegal.*

We are interested in developing a discourse with the explanatory power to help us interpret the reality produced by gore capitalism, founded in violence, (drug) trafficking and necropower, while at the same time presenting the dystopias[3] of globalization and its imposition. We are also interested in following the multiple threads that give rise to the capitalist practices underpinned by extreme and ultra-specialized forms of violence— practices that in certain geopolitical locales have become established as everyday forms of violence used to obtain recognition and economic legitimacy.

The raw nature of this violence obeys a logic born out of structures and processes planned in the very heart of neoliberalism, globalization and politics. We are talking about practices that are transgressive solely because their forcefulness makes the vulnerability of the human body clear, in how it is mutilated and desecrated. These practices constitute a scathing critique of the society of hyperconsumption, at the same time as they participate in it and in capitalism's inner workings, since:

> In many nations, organized crime has become a key political actor and an interest group, a player that must be taken into consideration by the legitimate political system. This criminal element frequently provides necessary foreign currency, jobs and the economic well-being essential for national stability, as well as the enrichment of those who hold political power (through at times corrupt means) especially in poor countries ... (Curbet, 2007, 63)

These practices have reached ever more shocking extremes with the advent of globalization, as it is founded on predatory logics that—along with *spectralization* and *speculation* in financial markets—foment and implement radically violent practices. In the words of Thomas Friedman, former special adviser to Secretary of State Madeleine Albright during the Clinton Administration:

> For globalization to work, America can't be afraid to act like the almighty superpower that it is ... The hidden hand of the market will never work without a hidden fist. McDonalds cannot flourish without McDonnell-Douglas, the designer of the F-15, and the hidden fist that keeps the world safe for Silicon Valley's technology is called the United States Army, Air Force, Navy and Marine Corps. (Curbet, 2007, 64)

Mary Louise Pratt further discusses globalization as a false protagonist:

> The term globalization eliminates understanding, even the desire for understanding. In this sense, globalization functions at times as a kind of false protagonist which impedes a sharper interrogation of the processes that have been reorganizing practices and meanings during the last 25 years. (Pratt, 2002, 1)

If we draw on this analysis, we could say that what we are designating here as gore capitalism is one of those processes of globalization, its B-side, unmasking the extent of its consequences. For this reason, we do not deny the complexity of the phenomenon and will inquire into the array of consequences that exceed the interpretative regime that undergirds capitalist monopoly.

In the same sense, given the existence of movements, discourses, and resistance activities that seek to confront the reach of capitalist discourse, we think it is vital to clarify that our reflections on gore capitalism do not share the assumptions of (nor are they limited to) capitalist discursive practices. We propose gore capitalism, then, as a heteroclite space that has not been sufficiently theorized within these alternatives to capitalism, which understand gore capitalism as strongly rooted in capitalist logic and so relegate it to the realm of the irrational, labeling it undesirable and dystopian.

In a similar way, the process of gore capitalism is rendered invisible by the discourse of the official capitalist economy and neglected within its system of thought; it is not considered especially significant or complex (despite its noteworthy explicatory functions), but rather it is relegated to consideration only as part of the black market and its effects on capital. However, now that the criminal economy is estimated to make up no less than 15% of global commerce,[4] the effects of gore capitalism on the world economy is evident; these numbers bestow it with real power in terms of planetary economic decisions.

The urgency of devising a critical discourse that describes gore capitalism derives in part from the need to have a common language with which to discuss the phenomenon, for it is well known that "the world reveals itself in language, and social relations are elaborated in language" (Heritage, 1984, 126).

As language is a core element in the epistemological organization of the world, we think it vital to investigate, review, reason through and attempt to propose an explanatory discourse that might provide us with a conceptual frame to think through, analyze and approach these spaces/fields and their practices. We also think it is essential to name these spaces/fields and their practices from a transfeminist perspective, by which we mean a network that opens discursive spaces and fields to all those contemporary practices and subjects that have not been directly analyzed. We are especially concerned with the lack of explanatory language for the phenomena we identify here with the term gore capitalism. We cannot ignore the relationships between legal and illegal economies and the rampant use of violence as a mode of capitalist *necroempowerment* and wealth accumulation. If we were to do so, we would neutralize the possibility of action against them and obscure the fact that these processes regularly impact the bodies of all those who are part of the *minority becoming—*

upon whom, one way or another, all of this brutal violence falls.

Thus, we propose an analysis of gore capitalism, understood as "the systematically uncontrolled and contradictory dimension of the neoliberal project" (Pratt, 2002, 2). It is a product of economic polarization, the excesses of information/advertising that create and support a hyperconsumerist identity and its counterpart: the ever-shrinking numbers of people with the financial power to satisfy their consumer desires. This process creates radical capitalist subjects we term *endriago subjects* (See Chapter 2) and new discursive figures that make up an *episteme of violence*, as well as reconfiguring the concept of work through a perverse sense of agency, now rooted in the necropolitical commercialization of murder. All of this is evidence of the dystopias produced through an unconsidered adherence to pacts with (masculinist) neoliberalism and its objectives.

Endriago subjectivities are created in the face of this world order, as individuals seek to establish themselves as valid subjects with the *possibility of belonging and ascending within society*. These subjects create new *fields*, out of one of the most ferocious, devastating and irreversible processes of capitalist investment. They contradict the logic of what is acceptable and normative because of their new awareness that they have become redundant in the economic order. These subjects confront their situation and their context by means of *necroempowerment* and the fugitive, dystopian *necro-practices* of gore, as they convert this process into the *only possible reality* and attempt to *legitimate* the processes of underground economies (black market, drug trafficking, weapons, bodies, etc.) through their reign of violence. These actions both create and reinterpret new fields apart from the *valid ones* and thereby wield influence over political, public, official, social and cultural processes.

As Pratt affirms, "Once again we live in a world of bandits and pirates,[5] now in the form of coyotes and polleros[6] [drug-traffickers, hitmen, kidnappers, etc] who work on the borders of the whole planet" (Pratt, 2002, 3).

It is no accident that drug trafficking is currently the largest industry in the world (followed by the legal economies of fossil fuels and tourism), that drug money flows freely through the arteries of global financial systems, or that drug trafficking is itself one of the clearest examples of gore capitalism.

It is clear that "this is not the scene we imagined for the beginning of the new millennium" (Pratt, 2002, 2), but it is the one we are faced with; it is our philosophical responsibility to analyze it in order to expose the weakness and inflexibility of discourses of globalization and neoliberalism, which are unable to explain these processes.

Contemporary history is no longer based on the experiences of survivors, but rather on the vast numbers of the dead. That is, the "litany of cadavers has been an answer to the clearly utopian character of the official discourses about globalization" (Pratt, 2002, 5), subverting the optimistic discourse of *flow* brought on by globalization, since now what flows *freely* is not people, but drugs, violence and the capital these produce.

This represents an inversion of terms, whereby life is no longer valued in and of itself but only as an object of monetary exchange in the market: a transvaluation whereby the only measure of value is the ability to mete out death to others. Necropower is exercised from unexpected quarters for the benefit of official power-holders.

The explosion of unrestrained and hyper-specialized violence is evidence of the lack of any (regulatable) future, along with the fact that in capitalism's interstices no one has anything to lose, because life is no longer important (which means the taboo against killing has been entirely undone). Violence continually iterated in the here and now makes it impossible to contemplate the idea of the *Future* in the ways the West has customarily done. The violence demands a reassessment of futurity itself.

Driven by capitalism's interpretive monopoly, ignorance and contempt for the Third World have taught us to see other elements and historical dynamics (those of the Others) as insignificant. Neglect and contempt have provoked a response born of silence and invisibility that seems at once unstoppable and unfathomably violent.

The result is a process of capitalism's deformed duplication, an unfolding of parallel identities in places, spaces, and subjects that incorporate, retranslate, and fuse together these experiences into something simultaneous, emancipatory, and fragmentary. We thus see that

> The incapacity of neoliberalism to generate belonging, collectivity and a believable sense of the future produces, among other things, enormous crises of existence and of meanings that are being lived by the non consumerists and consumerists of the world in forms that the neoliberal ideology can neither predict or control. (Pratt, 2002, 15)

It is precisely in this space where we encounter the relevance and importance of the following study.

A Clarification About Gore: Becoming-Snuff

Before going any further, we think it necessary to make a clear distinction between gore capitalism and snuff capitalism.[1] Both terms are borrowed from the taxonomy of cinematic genres[2] and posited here as categories that can be transposed to a philosophical context to allow us to analyze the contemporary *episteme of violence*, its logics and its practices.

We have elected to use the term gore capitalism instead of snuff capitalism, because this phenomenon of extreme violence as a tool used against bodies by the global economy—and especially by organized crime as a key component of that economy—does not fit the category of snuff. Rather, this situation fits well within the boundaries of gore, since it has retained the grotesque and parodic element of the spilling of blood and guts, which as it is so absurd and unjustified, would appear to be unreal, gimmicky and artificial, a shade below full fatality, a work-in-progress on the way to becoming snuff, that still leaves open the possibility of being curbed. Nonetheless, now we have observed that what we initially posited as gore capitalism is rapidly morphing into snuff capitalism.

1

The Breakdown of the State
as a Political Formation

> Ethics must not be unworthy of what happens to us.
> —Gilles Deleuze

The (Philosophical) Concern with Violence

Though violence as a behavior has been present since the beginnings of what we know as History, this phenomenon has not been sufficiently studied by philosophy, and those examinations have not been disseminated widely enough, except in isolated cases like Machiavelli or Hobbes for whom violence was a central topic of study. For the former, violence is understood as a crucial tool in the acquisition and consolidation of power (Machiavelli, 2004), and for the latter as a characteristic feature of the human condition and of "sociability" (Hobbes, 2003).

There are a number of contemporary theorists who engage with (or have engaged with) the issue of violence as a recurrent subject of their work: Georges Bataille, Slavoj Žižek, Judith Butler, Giorgio Agamben and Achille Mbembe. Nonetheless, philosophical concern with the topic is not immediately evident; this appears paradoxical in light of the fact that violence has intensified in the last century, becoming the decisive issue for the West and for contemporary life, and an essential interpretive paradigm for the present moment. As Charles Tilly explains:

> In absolute terms—and probably per capita as well—the twentieth century visited more collective violence on the world than any century of the previous ten thousand years. During the first half of the twentieth century, massive interstate wars produced most of the world's political deaths. [...] During the century's second half, civil war, guerrilla, separatist struggles, and conflicts between ethnically or religiously divided populations increasingly dominated the landscape of bloodletting. (Tilly, 2003, 55–6)

For this reason, the twentieth century can be understood as synonymous with violence; a violence that has been radicalized through neoliberalism and the advent of globalization until, by the first decade of the twenty-first century, it merits the label *gore reality*. At this point, it is reasonable to ask why this form of violence linked to gore capitalism is different from previous instantiations. The answer is found in a framework generated both by the execution of violence as well as by its spectacularization and subsequent commercialization in the news media. Within gore capitalism, violence is used simultaneously as a technology for control and as a *gag*—a political tool. We refer to a *gag* in the sense of the comic and theatrical tradition, especially pertaining to the circus: "a closed circuit of pure hilarity: it has to do with the very infantile and primitive taste for disruptive surprise and startling disorder, with the very instinctual pleasure found when things slip out of their places, fall or collapse unexpectedly" (Brieva, 2009, 1).

Violence and its spectacularization now cut across all fields of knowledge and action; it has become the preeminent model for the analysis of contemporary reality, as well as the fundamental driver of a *g-local episteme* that extends from the peripheries of the planet to the center and vice versa.

We understand *violence* to be an interpretive category with distinct incarnations, notably the version of violence that is intimately tied to actions. In other words, the concept of violence we are using includes both its actual, bloody utilization as well as its relationship with the media and the symbolic.

Now that violence has become an *episteme*, it is more necessary than ever to remember that philosophy "begins when the gods fall silent [and what is the frenzied violence of gore capitalism but a silence of the referent, an oblivion?]. Nonetheless, all philosophical activity consists of speech" (Lyotard, 1996, 121). Therefore, it is imperative that philosophy not forget its debt to discourse, the power it holds to create discourse, ideas and interpretations about the reality around us.

For this reason, a deeper philosophical investigation into violence is vital, now that it is indisputable that violence—as an (extremely effective) tool of the global economy—has generated something of its own discursive turn.

We understand this *episteme of violence* as the set of relations that joins our moment to the discursive and non-discursive practices that arise out of violence, creating epistemological figures that no longer have direct relationships with now-inadequate models for the interpretation of reality. Thus, we see a gap in the ethical agreements of the West and in the applicability of Western philosophical discourse to contemporary economic, social, political and cultural conditions.

Further, we propose that the combination of this *episteme of violence* with capitalism has created the phenomenon that we call gore capitalism. This phenomenon is born out of the state of exception[1] under which life unfolds in multiple parts of the planet, with special intensity in economically depressed nations known as the Third World and along the borders between these nations and the First World.

We stress that it is primarily in the Third World and along its borders where the effects of gore capitalism are most obvious and brutal. This assertion is grounded in our desire to show that despite the fact that gore practices—at least the most obvious ones—originate in the Third World, understanding the logic, processes and consequences of these practices demands that we map out conceptual bridges and develop a less exoticizing knowledge, one closer to the activities and demands of Third-Worldized reality. This Third-Worldized reality also provides information about what the First World is already facing and will continue to face. We are not suggesting that the phenomena taking place in those Third-Worldized spaces and the categories for their interpretation are universalizable, or that their validity and applicability can be assumed without taking geopolitical difference into account. Nonetheless, we can identify certain processes related to globalization and to the flow of criminal economic models that are beginning to emerge in First World societies. We see evidence of this in its news media and its consumption practices, which have begun to legitimate and reproduce violent, often criminal identities in film, music, videogames, art and literature.[2]

The First World lacks knowledge of this gore logic, not because it has never participated in criminality, but because this type of activity is linked to a logic of globalization that is still quite poorly understood and has unpredictable consequences. The lack of a set of common codes to decipher these gore practices has relegated us to an epistemological, theoretical and practical void.

The Breakdown of the Nation-State

First, following Foucault, we will attempt to theorize liberalism—the foundational doctrine for contemporary neoliberalism—by providing both a summary and a reflection on the rupture it implied for the *Reason of State* once it had ceased to be understood as a *Polizeiwissenschaft*.

The concept of *Polizeiwissenschaft* is posited by German scholars in the eighteenth century as a technology of governance that "attends to the problems of the populations: … health, birthrate, sanitation find an important place in it" (Foucault (1979b), 120). Foucault's reading of liberalism as a practice more than an ideology, "as a 'way of doing things' oriented toward [economic] objectives" (Foucault (1979b), 119), does away with the concept of the State as totalitarian and rational but also as beneficent.

Following this, the very notion of governability is undermined, as it is diminished by liberalism to a legal means to create "a political society founded on a contractual tie" and regulated by law, "because the law defines forms of general intervention excluding particular individual, or exceptional measures; and because the participation of the governed in the formulation of the law, in a parliamentary system, constitutes the most effective system of governmental economy" (Foucault (1979b), 121).

It is evident that the rights-oriented State guaranteed by law is governed by a liberal logic that affords freedom of action to the economically well-off. But freedom of action is not the exclusive property of those who hold economic power or are protected by the law because of that power. In fact, gore practices are not subject to the law but rather defy it and yet can still be understood through the framework of freedom of action. In the same way, practices of resistance justify themselves according to a logic of agency; they neither support the neoliberal system nor are they classifiable as gore practices, but rather are situated at a critical distance from both.

The liberal argument is for the creation of a State that neglects its responsibilities to society and its subjects, establishing a dynamic of subjects who are unidirectionally "subjected" within the framework of the law. That is, the system's demand that individuals take responsibility for themselves—

rendering the negotiation of their economic relations social and intersubjective, and in a certain sense, private—do not take into account those subjects who lack the power to negotiate from a non-disadvantaged position.

Neoliberalism in the United States goes even further than liberalism in that it represents a (successful) attempt to "extend the rationality of the market…to areas that are not primarily economic, for example, family and birth policy, or delinquency and penal policy" (Foucault, 1979b, 79) without taking into account that freedom in economic processes can produce social inequities.

This expansion of economic rationality into new arenas leads to a weak form of State government and its eventual outsourcing, making economics the driving factor for all of the activities of governance. As a consequence (and via globalization's insistence on deregulation), a double-standard arises that makes labor precarious globally and fosters the emergence of gore practices. In an effort to attain economic, gender and (ultimately) social legitimacy, these practices are enacted by subjects who attempt to comply with one of the foundations of liberalism: embodying the masculinist figure of *the self-made man*.

In this way, globalization—whose fundamental premises are based in neoliberalism—leads to and provides evidence of the breakdown of the State.

In the contemporary context, the State plays a largely ambivalent role as theoretically its role is founded on a global politics of neoliberal coexistence. But in the era of globalization, the State can be understood more as a worldwide interstate political entity that eliminates its economic borders while reinforcing its internal borders and beefing up its surveillance systems.

This proliferation of borders, surveillance and internal controls increases the costs, the boom and the demand for gore's goods: drug- and human-trafficking, contract killings, private security run by mafias, etc.

Nevertheless, the economic outsourcing of State functions does not reduce its power and control: "That is to say, in this new governmentality sketched by the économistes, the objective will still be to increase the state's forces..." (Foucault, 2008, 332).

The breakdown of the welfare State can be seen in the displacement of governmentality by the economy (legitimate and illegitimate transnational corporations that force the entire system to adopt the laws of the market), a shift that transforms the concept of the nation-state into the nation-market. That is to say, it transforms a political unit into an economic one—governed by the laws of exchange and corporate profits—and connected in multiple ways to the global market.

Nation-State / Nation-Market

In order to discuss the displacement of govern-mentality, we must ask ourselves how the idea of globalization emerged and became so widespread. While there are multiple answers to this question, we'll concentrate here on the neoliberal discrediting of ideology. In 1989, the U.S. American political scientist Francis Fukuyama published *The End of History and the Last Man*, which used a neoliberal reinterpretation of Hegel to argue that ideology and grand meta-narratives had reached their end with the fall of Communism.

Following this, we find ourselves on a fugitive line of History, where time has continued to move on and where the sole remaining paradigm for thought—the religion of absolute neoliberalism—encounters no obstacles. Thus, the fall of Communism, de-ideologization and de-historicization left a fertile ground for the emergence of globalization.

We understand globalization as the deregulation of all spheres, along with the maximum weakening of all political mediation for the exclusive benefit of the logic of the market. This includes:

1. A deregulated labor market.
2. Deterritorialization (international segmentation and decontextualization of each nation's sphere of influence).

3. Decodification of financial flows as a result of the increased application of neoliberal policies.

4. Strategies utilized to ensure that money moves at the speed of information (the marriage of economics and technology).

Nonetheless, neoliberal discourse presents globalization to society as a reality based in equality. In line with the dictum of *equal access to everything*,[3] this discourse insists on the acceptance of the market as the only field that equalizes everything, precisely because it instills artificially-naturalized needs that drive consumption without distinction.

It's important to emphasize that the marriage of economics, politics and globalization popularizes the use of new technologies, under the guise of eliminating borders and shortening distances, even if only virtually. But the goal of this marriage is the creation of an uncritical and hyperconsumerist social consciousness that rolls out the red carpet for overt systems of control and surveillance. The existence of these systems is thought to be logical, acceptable and demanded by society itself, thus transgressing and re-conditioning any notion of privacy or freedom and shaping a new idea of personal, national and social identity. The contemporary idea of the social can be understood as a conglomeration of autonomous individuals who share a determined space and time and who participate actively or passively (and to varying degrees) in a culture of hyperconsumption.

A culture of hyperconsumption is a logical consequence of the emergence of the new ruling class of business elites, and of their political practices. In present-day culture, there is no longer room for heroes, only publicists.

The breakdown of the State as a political entity is accompanied by a dismantling or commercial resignification of the concepts of nation and nationalism. In order to analyze this idea of nationalism we turn to Clifford Geertz, who defined it in a text from the 1970s as "amorphous, uncertainly focused, half-articulated, but for all that highly inflammable" (Geertz, 1978, 205). In addition, he divided nationalism into two distinct types of claims for legitimacy:

> 1. Essentialist: appeals to terms like tradition, cultural, national character, blood relation, language, etc.; and
> 2. Epochalist: appeals to the history of our time, its direction and its meaning.

The market appropriates each of these claims for legitimacy, absorbing them and subsequently returning them into discourse in a resignified form (Geertz, 1978, 204). Of course, this resignification obeys the logic of its own interests; it subtly institutes a new form of nationalism that appeals to the concepts of unity and identity through consumption of both material and symbolic goods. Once the logic of the market has rendered everything (even concepts) commercializable, the concepts of *nation* and *nationalism* can be converted into decorative cultural trinkets.

The concept of the nation-state is dismantled and replaced by the concept of the nation-market. This displacement is of the utmost importance, since "one of the things that everyone knows but that no one can quite think how to demonstrate is that a country's politics reflect the design of its culture" (Geertz, 1978, 162).

Although it is true that the nation-market is no longer limited geographically to a country, it is also true that the United States is the primary representative of neoliberalism. The U.S. takes its culture to every corner of the globe through technology, mass media, networking, advertising and consumption; creates consumerist desires even in those places where it is difficult to satisfy those desires legally; and strengthens and reinforces the Market as the New Nation that *unites us*.

It should be clarified that this discourse is not implanted in a direct or obvious way; on the contrary, it emerges in a sort of discursive sleight-of-hand, where the market terms are exchanged for those defined and defended from an identitarian and even nationalist perspective—an exchange that thus is posited as practically "natural." There is much care taken to ensure that the concept of nation-market does not become popular too fast, displacing those used by different nationalisms and/or nations. This strategy of retaining national discourse (but only in theory) uses it as a legitimizing cover for the consumerist discourse of the nation-market.

Nationalist discourse is encouraged and inflamed in order to dismantle or immobilize nations themselves, so that all activities are directly opened to the market. This is evidenced by the fact that the majority of European countries in which the political right is in power defend a neoliberal economy while simultaneously deploying a conservative discourse that appeals to nationalism.[4] Nonetheless, underlying the tenets of nationalism is the system of nation-market that imposes parameters of personal, cultural, social and international identity through the use of registered trademarks (™), logos (®), names (©), companies, popular iconography, theories and so on, a process that presupposes purchasing power in order to confer a *status quo* that serves as a model for identity.

So far we have examined the breakdown of the State and the dismantling of the concept of nation in the First World. But these same processes have taken a different direction in the Third World; there, the breakdown of the State has taken a dual form, divided between the adoption of neoliberal demands and the literal interpretation of these demands by Third World populations. The result has been the creation of an alternative State of hyperconsumerism and violence.

Narco-State

In the case of Mexico, we can see that the breakdown of the nation-state has been *sui generis*, given that the new State is not controlled by the government but by organized crime, primarily the drug cartels. Through the literal adoption of market logic and violence as a tool of empowerment, Mexico has become a narco-state.

What we are calling the narco-state is not a recent phenomenon; on the contrary, it's the result of a long and complex process. We could say that ever since the end of the 1970s, the Mexican state cannot be thought of as a state *per se*, but rather as a web of political corruption that has followed the orders of drug traffickers in the management of the country (Resa, 1999). This fusion of drug trafficking and politics has become even more extreme in the last decade, locking the government and organized crime in a constant battle for power.

The phenomenon of organized crime in Mexico must be contextualized by the fact that the gray or black market is the most reliable sector of the economy within the country. Organized crime was born out of a corrupt, dismantled State that led the population into chaos, and the people have accepted the criminal model as "a rational response to a highly unusual economic and social environment ... With the state in collapse and the security forces overwhelmed and unable to police, cooperating with the criminal culture was the only option" (Glenny, 2008, 55).

Organized crime thus becomes entangled with the state, taking over (or financing) many of its functions. This process gives rise to an inscrutable web that is difficult to challenge in any effective way, since the needs of the population are met by the creation of infrastructure funded by drug trafficking, including schools, hospitals, and more. The boundaries between the functions of the state and those of drug trafficking become blurred, a situation made more acute by the silence and dissimulation of citizens. As Carlos Resa Nestares has argued:

> It's clear that the economic power resulting from drug trafficking translates into social and political power. Corruption—and intimidation and violence when corruption fails—generates important returns as regards political decision-making, providing indirect access to debates about policies that impact [traffickers], allowing them to push for policies that favor them and on

occasion go against the interests of citizens. What's more, the rationally economic minds of the most powerful drug traffickers are not solely dedicated to developing effective plans for distribution and expansion, but also to expanding their own social legitimacy. Drugs generate employment and wealth in the most devastated parts of the First and Third Worlds, and this monetary flow can give rise to personal loyalties. But the most powerful drug traffickers also devote significant (though proportionally small) amounts of their income for social welfare and charity projects (Resa, 2003).[5]

During the economic crisis suffered by most Latin American countries in the 1980s, poverty became more extreme and the alliance between drug traffickers and politicians was strengthened, creating in Mexico and in many other Third World countries, "a Frankenstein that slipped out the door of the laboratory [of Chicago-school market economics] almost unnoticed" (Glenny, 2008, 56).

A number of factors played a role in popularizing the criminal economy and the use of violence as a tool of the market: price liberalization; market deregulation; declining support for the agricultural sector;[6] the dismantling and inefficiency of state functions; deficiencies in the enforcement of the most basic guarantees of human rights; spectralization of the market; advertising and information overload; constant frustration; and imposed workplace precarity. All of these factors fired the "the starting gun for a roller-coaster ride into the unknown" (Glenny, 2008, 56), a series of parallel measures that paved the way for gore capitalism.

In the 1990s, new reforms were enacted in the Mexican economy: the North American Free Trade Agreement between Mexico, the United States and Canada, which deepened the government's traditional subservience to foreign companies (especially those from the United States and Asian countries). NAFTA had a number of catastrophic shortcomings. The costs of basic foodstuffs and housing were liberalized, driving prices well beyond the means of millions of citizens; however, costs that impacted only a small minority of business owners (like oil and natural gas) were unaffected. This brought absolute political and economic devastation to the country, making the middle class an ever-shrinking sector of the population. Its shrinkage and the corresponding rise in social inequality—the result of policies that gave foreign and (a few) Mexican companies "a license to print money" (Glenn, 2008, 56)—led to defiance of the laws and efforts to seize a piece of the pie through the illegal economy. The price of this almost instantaneous wealth was bloodshed and loss of life; yet the price does not seem too high in a context where life is not worth living, in a situation of hyper-precarity, constant frustration, and grinding poverty irreversible by any other means.

"By normal standards one might perceive extortion, kidnapping, and murder as constituting a rather harsh policing regime; and most people would probably find it hard to approve of car theft, narcotics, or sex trafficking as a legitimate business enterprise" (Glenn, 2008, 61). But Mexico and the majority of Latin America are not in a normal situation. Despite its size and wealth of resources, Mexico has seen mass migration from the countryside to the city and multiple devaluations of the currency, and its government has proven incapable of adapting to decisive changes in the world economy in a non-subservient fashion. With these developments, it becomes clear that this society cannot have any say over "exceptional opportunities [that become available to] the quick-witted, the strong or the fortunate (oligarchs, criminals, bureaucrats whose power is suddenly detached from state control)" (Glenny, 2008, 61).

The Mexican Government's Fight Against Drugs

As we have discussed, drug trafficking and criminality in Mexico make contributions to the state in numerous ways. These sources not only account for a large percentage of the nation's GDP, but the state also benefits from the fear instilled in the population by criminal organizations, capitalizing on the *effectiveness of fear*[7] to declare the country in a *state of exception* (Agamben, 2003). In this way, the state justifies the abridgement of rights and the imposition of ever more invasive authoritarian measures and security initiatives. In addition, by declaring the country to be in a *state of exception*, it justifies the dismantling of the welfare state and the elimination of social resources as the price that must be paid to guarantee security.

The Mexican government and its security forces do not seek to put an end to the reign of the drug cartels, but rather to delimit them and use them to their own advantage as they have done for the last forty years. Implementing effective strategies to fight against drug trafficking in Mexico—and in all the countries deeply dependent on drug cartels—would have a recessionary impact on the economy as a whole and lead to significant social consequences (Resa, 2001). As support for this assertion, we cite a number of excerpts from an interview with then Mexican Attorney General Eduardo Medina Mora conducted by Pablo Ordaz and published in *El País* on November 23, 2008:

PABLO DÍAZ: Not long ago, a cartoon was published in a Mexican newspaper featuring the Devil, looking very concerned, chatting with a colleague about the violent period the country was experiencing. "For decades," he said, "we were afraid Mexico would turn into Colombia. Now what scares us is that Hell will turn into Mexico..."

EDUARDO MEDINA MORA: I don't want to dismiss the size of the problem, since it is quite serious and we see it that way, but one must accept that the levels of violence in the country compared with other countries are not that unfavorable [sic] (Ordaz, 2008).

It is surprising to read that for Mexico's Attorney General the 5,300 murders recorded in 2008 are not enough to cause alarm, despite the state of undeclared war in a nation dominated by drug cartels. Perhaps the machinations of the government's fight against drug trafficking are consistent with a bloody project of eugenics, one in which minor players are slaughtered in order to teach the population a lesson and to regain respect as an institution, since it has lost so much ground over the years in the eyes of Mexican society. Perhaps what we are seeing is more a fight to regain the *state's honor* than a project to protect or guarantee the human and civil rights of Mexicans.

EDUARDO MEDINA MORA: The government's approach is not to put an end to drug trafficking, since we know there will always be a demand for illegal substances; rather, we want to strip these organizations of their enormous power of intimidation, the enormous firepower that they have built up over the years and their corresponding ability to destroy institutions...

As Medina Mora explains it, the principal approach in the fight against drug trafficking is to regain the *effectiveness of fear* as a power restricted to the state; that the power to terrorize and to benefit from that terror must belong to the government alone. In his statements, Medina Mora does not discuss a reformulation of the application of power, but rather his comments betray an authoritarian and even anti-democratic point of view. Neither does he pause to analyze the links that exist between these criminals and the construction of the Mexican nation based on machismo and the violence implied by that connection.

In this regard, Carlos Monsiváis tells us that the term *macho* is highly implicated in the state's construction of Mexican identity. The term gained widespread use in post-revolutionary Mexico as a sign of national identity (see Monsiváis, 1981, 9–20). During this period, the term *machismo* was associated with the peasantry and the working class; in the incipient Mexican nation, *macho* became an intensification of the concept of manliness that later would become naturalized as a *national heritage.* By that point, it no longer belonged solely to the subaltern classes, as machismo came to signify for all an "indifference when faced with death, contempt for feminine virtues and the affirmation of authority at all levels" (Monsiváis, 1981, 9). In Mexico, gender constructions are intimately tied to the construction of the state. Thus, in the contemporary context of the breakdown of the Mexican state, we must highlight the connections between the State and the criminal class, as both uphold a violent kind of masculinity linked to the construction of the idea of the national. The political, economic and social consequences of this fact include a costly toll in human life due to the masculinist logic of defiance and the struggle for power. If this continues, it will legitimate a criminal class as having an absolute right to commit violent acts, one of the key modes of compliance with the demands of hegemonic masculinity and national machismo.

In this interview, the fight against organized crime seems more like a settling of scores between powerful, damaged machos looking to avenge their honor and protect their territory. They seem unconcerned with the real consequences of the violence[8] and with the fear it causes in a civilian population attacked on two fronts: both by the clashes between organized gangs and by the occupation of public spaces by the Mexican armed forces. The result is an endemic fear that shows up across nearly the entire country, evidenced by civilians confined to their houses, prisoners of a feeling of vulnerability and a sense of (not entirely justified) guilt. At the same time, criminals roam freely and with complete peace of mind throughout the country, and the government is spared any active civil demonstrations that might demand it fulfill its responsibilities to guarantee security.

The danger of this ever-growing fear is that the paranoia, the feeling of abandonment, chronic stress, and constant terror might lead to an outbreak of civil unrest that would culminate in the overthrow of the state due to its incompetence, and end in civil war. Under such circumstances, "you become a beast. And then you're really on the edge … Faced with dead bodies, there's nothing else to do but fight … The problem is that no one can afford to think he's not involved. It's not enough to assume that the way you live your life will protect you from every danger. It's no longer enough to say, 'They're killing each other'" (Saviano, 2008, 86, 78, 91). But the Attorney General's real problem with violence is not that it is being used, but that it is not being used by the state:

EDUARDO MEDINA MORA:: President Felipe Calderón has said that the criminal organizations in some of those areas [along Mexico's northern border] have vied with the state for control over its basic powers: the exclusive right to the legitimate use of force, the exclusive right to levy taxes and, on certain occasions, the exclusive right to issue general purpose regulations.

What President Felipe Calderón did not say is that since the rule of the PRI and during the two PAN governments,[9] drug traffickers have rivaled the state in the creation of infrastructure, jobs and schools. He did not say a single word about the inexorable logic with which corrupt bureaucrats, politicians and police have justified their pandering to those with financial power—whether they be business owners, criminals or both. We know the decision to let oneself be corrupted is not a difficult one to make when the only visible alternative is poverty and economic stagnation. What is difficult in such circumstances is to resist the temptation of consumerism.

The war against drug trafficking being waged by the Mexican state makes clear that:

[Whoever looks for] solutions based on the greater engagement of the police or military alone betray[s] a profound abdication of political responsibility. They are the product of unimaginative politicians who lack either the vision or the interest to address the great structural inequities in the global economy upon which crime and instability thrive. (Glenny, 2008, 345)

What official discourses do not say is that in Mexico the drug cartels will not be able to be effectively eradicated as long as structural inequalities persist among the population; as long as the "lack of work [continues and presents us with] the impossibility of finding a way to earn a living—other than emigrating" (Saviano, 2008, 68); until the concepts of *modernity* and *progress* are effectively deconstructed and cease to be used as guideposts for political discourse; until that discourse incorporates real possibilities of a geographically-relevant politics; as long as we remain stuck in the spectacle of violence and the celebration of hyperconsumerism; as long as we fail to question a political discourse based on male supremacy that requires the display of violence as an element of masculine self-affirmation; and above all as long as sustainable, long-term economic stability remains elusive.

Drug Trafficking and the US American Psyche

As we have seen, the imbrication of Mexican politics with the criminal economy has led to a situation in which "a subject has been instated at the national level, a sovereign and extra-legal subject, a violent and self-centered subject; its actions constitute the building of a subject that seeks to restore and maintain its mastery through ... systematic destruction" (Butler, 2006, 68).

Judith Butler's words express her understanding of the *psyche of the U.S. government* (under the administration of George W. Bush). It is no accident that one can trace numerous parallels between this psyche and that of Mexico's organized criminal drug trade, since these two apparently antagonistic worlds are in fact comparable in several ways.

There are two integral similarities are worth mentioning here. First is the use of extreme violence as a primary means of obtaining and retaining a territory (the U.S. war in Iraq is a recent example of this, though it is apparent in the country's constant waging of war; in the case of the drug cartels, there is the internal fighting, as well as clashes with the police and anti-drug authorities). In both cases, the goal is also the procurement and free circulation of a product (oil and drugs, respectively) in order to secure a market that guarantees them exponential growth in profits, yielding even greater power and legitimating their participation and supremacy in the logic of the market, the patriarchy,[10] and international capitalism. The second similarity is their shared attachment to quasi-illegal strategies as a direct means of exercising unrestricted power for individual benefit. "Illegality works outside of the law, but at the service of power, of the rule of the law, of the economy's rule and law, replicating power structures and reproducing them" (Butler, 2008).

There is a close relationship between the demands of the legal economy and the creation and flourishing of the black market. In other words, the different structures of illegality function at the behest of legality; many forms of illegal action are born of and protected by the stamp of legality. We will provide one example: Misha Glenny recounts in her book *McMafia* that the U.S. offered extremely generous financial and economic support to the countries of Eastern Europe after the fall of communism, "support oriented toward the creation and maintenance of illegal organizations which would dedicate themselves to the production of drugs, arms, and high-tech, products they would later sell all over the world" (Glenny, 2008, 11). As the example makes clear, the borders between legal and underground economies are blurred. As Glenny writes, "In both banking and commodity trading, the criminal operates much closer to home than we think" (Glenny, 2008, xvii).

It is therefore not surprising that—in light of the economic demands of the New World

Order—organized crime has globalized its own activities so that now there is a web of almost imperceptible connections between legal and illegal economies. The fact is that:

> criminal organizations of five continents have appropriated the "spirit of world cooperation" and participate as partners in the conquest of new markets. They invest in legal businesses not only to launder dirty money but also to acquire the capital required for their illegal businesses. Their preferred sectors: high-rent real estate, leisure, the media, and … banking. (Subcomandante Marcos, 1997)

It is a well-known fact that many forms of economic and political illegality are recognized and accepted by the state. Organized crime has deeply penetrated the politics and economy of the nation-state, to the extent that it now can boast of being a subset of the modern economy. "Here, then, is the rectangular mirror in which legality and illegality exchange reflections. On which side of the mirror is the criminal? On which side the pursuer?" (Subcomandante Marcos, 1997)

So it is theoretically comprehensible that the logics of illegality (drug trafficking, the mafia) should so nearly approximate those of the U.S.

neoliberal state, since the structures of the mafia directly reproduce those structures of power.

This same state makes constant covert use of illegal goods and services, thus creating a constant demand for them. Obligated to comply with the logic of capitalism, these subjects have made new commodities out of an endless number of things that previously would not have been seen as marketable: drugs, weapons, bodies, contract killers, etc. The result is:

> [a crass] marketing campaign designed to repackage a way of relating to one another that had been tarnished with the stamp of radical capitalism and had until quite recently (and logically) been anathema to the majority of the planet's inhabitants (Estévez & Taibo (2008), 354).

This leads us to ask ourselves what strategies should be adopted when violence has *become* the law of the market, inverting the usual relationship between these terms: until now it had been the market that set the rules for the use of violence. Since gore capitalism has already emerged, been embraced, and normalized, can the categories of *legitimacy* and *illegitimacy* remain valid in describing the use of violence? What makes violence something legitimate? What is the price exacted from us for exercising it? Violence is no longer the exclusive property or monopoly of the nation-state. The monopoly on violence has been put up for auction, and organized crime is making the highest bid.

Economic Entrepreneurs, Political Entrepreneurs and Violence Specialists

Since "criminals, organized and disorganized ... [are] good capitalists and entrepreneurs, intent on obeying the laws of supply and demand" (Glenny, 2008, xiii), we should investigate the concept of *entrepreneur*—a key element in the construction and triumph of capitalist logic.

According to a manual of business management, an entrepreneur is "someone who identifies an opportunity and organizes the necessary resources to put it into operation."[11] It's common to use this term to refer to someone who creates a company, finds a business opportunity, or starts up a venture under their own initiative.

We can see that the term *entrepreneur* is used to positively designate those subjects who have decided to make an active incursion into the economy. But in this definition of entrepreneur, based on following neoliberal logic, we find no restrictions on the type of companies the entrepreneur can create. This omission allows us to intuit that there are literally no commercial restrictions in this regard; any type of business can be created. In other words, as long as profits are produced, the business is legitimated economically, and though a certain minimum level of ethics might be assumed, those ethics are never mentioned explicitly. Thus a discursive vacuum is created for the interpretation and practice of the concept of entrepreneurship.

If we analyze the endriago subjects of the criminal economy according to the rules of the market (and not according to the media's spectacularized vision of them), they become perfectly valid, even legitimate, entrepreneurs who strengthen "the pillars of the economy, the hidden mine where the beating heart of the market gets its energy" (Saviano, 2008, 123).

Some of the distinctive characteristics of the entrepreneur are innovation, flexibility, dynamism, a willingness to take risks, creativity and orientation toward growth. Under this rubric, the endriago subject—that is, the *entrepreneurs of gore capitalism*—can be understood as a new creature, an amalgam of *economic entrepreneur*, *political entrepreneur* and *violence specialist*.

This amalgam demands that one entrepreneur have knowledge of several fields or have connections to them. The *economic entrepreneur* must know how to perform the functions of the *political entrepreneur*, who specializes primarily in "activating (and sometimes deactivating) boundaries [the boundaries between us and them], stories, and relations ... [in such a way as to] wield significant influence over the presence, absence, form, loci, and intensity of ... violence" (Tilly, 34). This is a task of supreme importance in the flourishing of the criminal economy. If economic entrepreneurs do not have such knowledge then they must contract with individuals who do. Additionally, they must have violence specialists on their payroll; these individuals control the means for inflicting damage on people or objects through the use of force and the mercilessly efficient techniques that aid them in maintaining or seizing power.

In the entrepreneurial criminal economy, this amalgam of political figures is intersectional and is often represented by "leaders of mercenaries, international weapons merchants, regional warlords, military rulers, and many a political ruler who disposes of his or her own armed force" (Tilly, 36). Disposing of one's own armed force is one of the many conditions met by the Mexican drug cartels.

It's important to underscore that within this criminal web the *violence specialists* occupy a liminal space where it is not always possible to separate their work from that of the government's security forces. In fact, it is well known that "specialists in inflicting damage (such as police, soldiers, guards, thugs and gangs) play significant parts in collective violence," and that many of these figures are employed by the state or otherwise entangled in it (Tilly, 4–5).

The Zetas—former soldiers from the Mexican and Salvadoran armies who constitute the private army for the Gulf Cartel—are one example of such violence specialists. Their use of violence has become famous for being tremendously effective, theatrical and ruthless. For example, they are known for their live video-taped decapitations of their victims or enemies that are then uploaded to YouTube along with oral or written messages with threats.

The fact that these violence experts have been trained by governments explodes any simple division between the *insurgents* and the *forces of order*; it re-signifies these categories and creates new ones. In this new territory, violence-related expertise has been converted into merchandise governed by a commercial logic of supply and demand.

Through this commercial logic, the Mexican cartels have effectively created an alternative state with its own powers and recruitment techniques. These range from the most rudimentary, like displaying *narcomantas* (narco-banners),[12] to transnational pirate radio that broadcasts messages like this one:

We would like to invite all citizens who have served in the military and who have attained the rank of *kaibil* [elite military forces] to provide security for vehicles transporting goods into Mexico. We offer opportunities for advancement. Interested? Please call…. (*Independiente*, 2008)

These recruitment techniques, which from some perspectives could seem like ridiculous jokes, are anything but. They have been undertaken in all seriousness and with absolute impunity from a literal interpretation of capitalism, in doing so reshaping the roles and activities of violence. They have reconfigured the system of production and re-conceptualized work itself, via a dystopian resignification that makes the techniques of the violence specialist not just a *normal job* but a *desirable* one, offering "opportunities for advancement" in the context of the global rise of labor precarity.

As an example of this paradigm shift, consider the case of a contract killer who specialized in dissolving the debtors and enemies of the Tijuana cartel boss in acid. This individual was caught on the Tijuana border on January 24, 2009. After his capture, he testified at his first hearing that he had dissolved three hundred bodies in acid, and that his job was "an ordinary job," according to his statement, a job for which he received $600 per week. Of course, the increasing levels of labor precarity do not solely affect Third World countries, but it has also become a feature of the nerve centers of economic power, coexisting alongside opulence.

In First World Europe, we can see a clear demonstration of this in Naples, where gore practices are also understood to fall within the rubric of work. According to Roberto Saviano, the word *piece* has also come to mean a murder: "*To make a piece*: an expression taken from contract labor or piecework. Killing a human being became the equivalent of manufacturing something, it didn't matter what. A piece" (Saviano, 2008, 103).

2

Capitalism as Cultural Construction

> We dreamed of utopia and woke up screaming.
> —Roberto Bolaño

A fundamental question traverses this book: what has happened to work? As we saw in the section on *economic entrepreneurs*, the concept of work itself has been reshaped. As gore practices have disrupted the Marxist model of production and consumption, work has undergone a radical change comparable in scope to the changes wrought by the industrial revolution. The objective lack Marx referred to and used as the basis for his theory of the state, class struggle, and the division of labor has been disrupted by the technological and electronic revolutions of the last thirty years.

[W]e have witnessed a radical departure from empire, from domination and from need, and we have entered the realm of abundance. And the tragic paradox that marks our era is that for the first time, a utopia of happiness would in fact be possible on earth ... but we are experiencing a re-feudalization of the world, the concentration of wealth in the oligarchies of finance capitalism, now infinitely more powerful than all other forces on the planet. (Estévez and Taibo, 2008, 111–112)

As Ziegler argues, that vision of utopia has been obscured and has moved even further out of reach because of the radicalization of capitalism in its neofeudalist form along with the emergence of the phenomenon of hyper-violence, which has intensified in recent years. These shifts have given rise to what we call gore practices, which signal the advent of gore capitalism.

This form of capitalism is now found in all of the so-called Third World countries as well as throughout Eastern Europe. It is close to breaching and taking up residence in the nerve centers of power, otherwise known as the First World. It is crucial to analyze gore capitalism because, sooner or later, it will end up affecting the First World; since globalization makes the world smaller in many respects, it is undeniable that if "we now inhabit a global village, there can be no salvation for a tiny minority of humanity" (Estévez and Taibo, 2008, 290). Gore capitalism tells us that

nothing is untouchable and that all taboos of economics and of respect for life have been shattered.
There is no longer any space for restrictions or for
salvation; all of us will be affected.

The question of capitalism's transformation
into gore is not a question in isolation, rather it
encompasses the entirety of capitalism. Thus, it is
necessary to approach it with a comprehensive
vision, understanding it as a global phenomenon
and analyzing it from a variety of angles.

First, it is of primary importance to stress that
capitalism, in addition to being a system of production, has become a cultural construction as
well. This point is crucial, since our analyses will
not be solely focused on economics, but also on
capitalism's effects as a biointegrated cultural
construction.

> Consumer capitalism was not born automatically
> from industrial technologies capable of the mass
> production of standardized commodities. It is also
> a cultural and social construction that required the
> *education* of consumers and the visionary spirit
> of the creative entrepreneurs, the *visible hand of
> management.* (Lipovetsky, 2007, 24)

Although the transformation of capitalism is a historical fact and has been theorized from economic,
social, and now even virtual perspectives, it is also

the case that in recent decades there has been a break with past analyses. Capitalism has transcended its theoretical confines to become pure reality, physically palpable, and so close to us in space and time as to make its theorization difficult.

Given the difficulty of creating genealogies for a phenomenon and a term that refers to contemporary reality, we are forced to rely on a borrowed genealogy in order to cast a few relevant buoys into gore capitalism's ocean of discourse.

Thus, in line with Paul B. Preciado,[1] we will locate the first buoy in the post-Fordist era following the energy crisis and the decline of assembly-line production. These years were marked by the search for "new growth sectors in a transformed global economy. This is when 'experts' began talking about biochemical, electronic, computing, or communications industries as new industrial props of capitalism" (Preciado, 24). Preciado explicitly identifies the theoretical-conceptual-explanatory insufficiency of these discourses to explain the production of value and life in contemporary society: "We must first elaborate a new philosophical concept [gore] … that is equivalent to the force of work in the domain of classical economics" (Preciado, 41). In gore capitalism, the force of work is replaced by gore practices, understood as the systematic and repeated use of the most explicit forms of violence to produce capital.

Preciado also maps out a "cartography of the transformations in industrial production during the previous century, using as an axis the political and technical management of the body, sex, and identity" (Preciado, 24). We add to this the management of violence both by authorized entities (the state) and by those unauthorized Others who appropriate that power of management—through the use of violence on an array of individual bodies—without ever belonging to the *legitimate* system of management and capital-generating activities. Alongside this new research into the transformation of the global economy, we can begin to trace a line to track the establishment and expansion of gore capitalism.

The process of conceptualization begins with several phenomena converging: the subversion of traditional means of generating capital, a growing contempt for working-class people and their cultures, the rejection of politics and the rising number of disadvantaged people both in the Third World and in the peripheral sectors of the great economic centers.

These phenomena have coincided with increasing *socialization through consumption*—which has become the only way to maintain social ties—and the fact that "consumerist attitudes and pressures do not stop at the boundaries of poverty but instead extend to all social levels, even to those living on social security" (Lipovetsky, 2007, 185). In addition, we also have seen "the deculpabilization, trivialization [and the heroification] of crime in zones of social exclusion" (Lipovetsky, 2007, 184), as well as a drastic increase of media, entertainment, decorative violence, and the biomarket. These phenomena lead directly to gore practices as a legitimate and logical outcome of the evolution of the society of hyperconsumption. Violence and criminal activities are no longer seen as an *ethically dystopian* path, but as strategies available to everyone; violence comes to be understood as a tool to acquire money that allows individuals to purchase both commercial goods and social status.

With the dismantling of the traditional concept of work, masculinist ideology's insistence on the role of the *male provider* is threatened.[2] Precarious labor comes to be seen as a disgrace, as Roberto Saviano argues:

To work as an errand boy, waiter, or on a construction site is considered a disgrace [in the poorest neighborhoods of Naples]. In addition to the usual, eternal reasons—no contract, no sick days or vacation, ten-hour shifts—there's no hope of bettering your situation. The System [the term the Neapolitan Comorra uses for itself] at least grants the illusion that commitment will be recognized, that it's possible to make a career. An affiliate will never be seen as an errand boy, and girls will never feel they are being courted by a failure. (Saviano, 2008, 109)

It is precisely this conjunction of factors that will subsequently make gore capitalism (though that name is not used) inseparable (as it is today) from gore practices. These violent practices are part of the production of capital and are rooted in the consumerist education of our society of hyperconsumption, deregulation in the social and economic realms, and the *sexual division of work* (see Carrasco, 2003).

We do not mean to suggest that violence as a strategy for the quick acquisition of wealth has not existed in other periods. But the point is that this strategy has intensified as a result of the crisis in the great economic axes, known as the First World (or world economic powers). This imbalance in the axes of power creates an anti-Doppler effect, a swelling wave that directly impacts the so-called Third World, the territories furthest from these centers. While these effects are immediately felt in the centers of power, the responses from the furthest reaches are seen not as a spontaneous phenomenon, but as a direct response to the post-Fordist crisis. This crisis has already been largely forgotten in the center, but its effects are still apparent in other parts of the world. Where they are visible, multiple crises have had a cumulative effect; the responses to these crises have created social and economic dynamics like gore capitalism.

Third World responses to contemporary economic demands lead to the creation of an underlying order that makes violence a tool of production and then globalizes it. Gore capitalism could thus be understood as part of an intercontinental struggle of extreme post-colonialism, in which territory is recolonized via the desires for consumption, self-affirmation, and empowerment.

The logical way to explain the economic trends that create dystopian subjects and activities (to be referred to as endriago subjects and gore practices) does not allow for a moralistic approach. Instead, we analyze phenomena that first shatter and then remake the postulates of humanism that were meaningful to a society structured by the discourse of the welfare state, but has ceased to be useful in the contemporary world structured around the dictatorship of hyperconsumption. Thus, one of the fundamental changes wrought by the contemporary economic order (that is, globalization) centers on the very understanding of the concept of work, and consequently its brutal deregulation.

As a result of the rise of extreme workplace precarity and neglect of the countryside by both government and business, we see two notable consequences, taking into account that agriculture is a productive sector that generates neither quick nor particularly high profits. First, we are faced with the massive migration from the countryside to the cities, throwing the system out of balance and rendering it nonviable over the mid- and long-term. This drives the expansion of the precariat, which is so marginal as to no longer be encompassed by the term *poverty*, because:

> Until recently *poverty* described traditionally stable and identifiable social groups that were able to subsist thanks to local solidarities. This era is over: the repudiated populations of post-industrial society no longer constitute, properly speaking, a fixed social class. The landscape of hypermodern social exclusion is an incoherent nebula of particular situations and social routes. In this pluri-dimensional constellation there is no class-consciousness, group solidarity, or sense of common destiny, only clusters of very different personal stories and trajectories. Victims of social invalidation and of individual difficulties and situations, the new *unaffiliated* emerge in a society at once brutally unequal and hyper-individualist— a society, in other words, that has been liberated from the sociocultural framework of traditional class structures. (Lipovetsky, 2007, 182)

This *liberation* from traditional class structures makes it harder to achieve real socialization and cohesion, thus blocking any effective, critical resistance. Another consequence of business and governmental neglect of the countryside is that drug trafficking has become a terribly tempting and profitable work option, since at present the cartels are overwhelmingly powerful and possess sufficient economic and political resources to counter the state, to offer jobs, and to increase the value of the countryside itself.

The lack of social affiliation and the increasing availability of criminal employment mean that new conceptions of work are completely separated from ethical and humanist considerations, both within the corporate and the illegal economy.

Let's look at two clear examples of this break from ethical and humanist standards. First, in the context of the legal economy, the pharmaceutical industry's privatization and commercialization of medicines that could save millions of lives demonstrates clearly that the industry privileges economic profits over respect for human life. Second, in the context of the illegal economy, criminal organizations follow the same business logic as legal companies—seeking the highest profits and ignoring human costs—and benefit additionally from the symbolic and material profitability generated by the spectacularization of violence. Concretely, drug trafficking has re-conceptualized work itself, linking it with ideologies of hyperconsumption and individual reaffirmation, while concurrently upholding gender-related demands made on men, especially in the field of work.

Drug trafficking is rooted in the *revaluation* of the countryside as raw material for the creating of its product. At the same time, its indoctrination into consumerism leads to the use of violence as a tool to satisfy consumer needs and to affirm itself as a relevant actor. The ample purchasing power of drug traffickers legitimates their existence, transforms them into economically acceptable subjects, and re-affirms them within gender-based narratives that position men as *macho providers* and reinforce their virility through the active exercise of violence. In other words, traffickers become acceptable subjects both economically and socially, because they participate in the logics of the contemporary economy as wealthy hyperconsumers. Yet this participation takes place on *the dark side of the economy*, a fact that the State harshly condemns because it lies outside of its own financial control. For this reason, states see drug trafficking as the enemy because they evade paying taxes, a fact that gives rise to sizable economic losses for the capitalist system.

The economy of drug trafficking re-conceptualizes the market, tools for work, the concept of work itself and, fundamentally, the value of the countryside. Lorena Mancilla gets to the heart of the matter.

> I remember how Marxists always tried unsuccessfully to connect the urban struggle with the campesino [rural peasant] struggle, but now the *narco* [drug cartels] have produced a well-organized urban guerrilla. They have their own training centers (yesterday they found one in a basement in a house in Tijuana) and their own weaponry; they have strongholds disguised as houses in strategic locations. Their forces can sustain a three-hour firefight with the army as well as state, federal, and municipal police. All of this is the consequence of a campesino struggle, since drugs are produced in rural areas. It's interesting because we are talking about a campesino rebellion that consequently produces an urban guerrilla. Another interesting thing is that normally these types of movements happen in a single part of the world, or in a single country, but in this case the phenomenon occurs in countries where drugs are produced, countries drugs are transported through, and countries where drugs are consumed. We are talking about a disorganized international (perhaps intercontinental) revolution, without theorists at the reins, without heroes or flags, without demonstrations or uniforms or

heroic stories of little boats arriving to inhospitable shores, without ideals—a revolution with purely economic aims, set to music by the stuttering of automatic weapons and by the *corridos norteños* that memorialize key figures and battles. (Mancilla, 2008)

Mancilla's analysis leads us to consider how the phenomenon of drug-related violence re-conceptualizes the class struggle and paves the way to an extreme form of post-colonialism. It is a post-colonialism that has been recolonized by hyper-consumerism and frustration, a consequence of the economic conditions that dominate the contemporary world. In this struggle, the intermediaries have been eliminated, giving way to endriago subjects who act in radical and illegitimate ways for their own self-affirmation.

It is important to stress then that the genealogy of gore capitalism can be traced through processes initiated in the world's economic powers and through their demands on the world as a whole. Gore capitalism is a direct consequence of the transformation of First World capitalism through globalization. Globalization's practices are difficult to theorize because they have become unavoidable in a world ruled by the characteristics of the global financial market: the fluid, the euphemistic, the deferred, the spectral. Discursive reality itself is created through these same characteristics. At the same time, "the society of hyperconsumption is characterized by the increased search for commercial experiences to move and distract us—a search haunted by the experience of the *almost never* and the fear of *diminishing returns*" (Lipovetsky, 2007, 180–181).

The logic and the economic evolution of this type of capitalism makes it philosophically relevant to analyze both the system and how it informs a global epistemology related to the search for meaning and the production of narratives or discursive innovations that create new categories of thought. Through the establishment of hyperconsumption, capitalism—as the sole relational logic on the horizon, both materially and epistemologically—creates a neo-ontology that re-posits the fundamental questions of any subject: Who am I? What is the meaning of my existence? What place do I occupy in the world? Why? The response to these questions is founded on an obsession with consumption, combined with the human need to produce, to create and to make, a need studied by anthropologists.

All of this paves the way for the integration of this logic of consumer-action as something that cannot be confronted or eliminated, but that is being hybridized and naturalized, allowing our own bodies to be invaded by this logic. Overall, we could call this phenomenon the creation of the *biomarket*.

It is also relevant to ask how extreme violence, gender, death and thanatopolitics have been converted into a new form of fierce and unapologetic capitalism. How have these endriago subjects decided to participate in the world market and how have they empowered themselves in the parallel criminal economy sustained by the formal economy? How have these endriago subjects decided on a "certain individualistic rivalry, one of brutality, defiance and risk-taking" (Lipovetsky, 2007, 189)? These questions find their responses in a society that deifies mediatized (controlled?) violence and whose major economic powers—to take the specific case of the U.S.—rely on the arms race (which today exists in a modality which we will discuss later as *decorative violence*), warfare, and the power to dispense death (or refrain from dispensing it) to all those bodies-subjects-territories or capitals that dissent from their actions.

The more that general material conditions improve, the more subjectivization-psychologization of poverty intensifies. In a hyperconsumerist society, economic precarity doesn't just engender widespread material privations, but it also foments moral suffering, shame of being different, individual self-deprecation, and a feedback loop of negativity. The abrupt reappearance of exterior unhappiness advances in parallel with interior or existential happiness. (Lipovetsky, 2007, 191)

Given this context, it is logical that oppressed subjects begin to question the coherence and infallibility of the order imposed on them. Subsequently, they begin to lay claim to a form of empowerment, to use their destructive capacities as an engine of wealth creation by means of a transgressive subjectivity that coincides neither with the *subjectivity of the victors* nor of the defeated. This new subjectivity exceeds the frameworks of our theorizations of contemporary subjectivities, creating an endriago subjectivity based on "seeking out modes of illegitimate action and self-affirmation in order to exorcize the image and condition of victimhood," actions that provoke "calls for order and repression" (Lipovetsky, 2007, 189).

Capitalism in its gore version thus emerges not only from overexposure to televised violence or the violence of video games like *Grand Theft Auto* but also from poverty, since *the economy is itself a form of violence.* Nonetheless, this form of violence is not just explicit, but also insinuates itself into our bodies in a subtle and sanitized form, wrapped in inoffensive packaging and advertising that confronts us with our own inability to consume everything and eventually leads to constant frustration, and, in turn, to outright aggressiveness and further violence. As Gilles Lipovetsky explains:

> Television's impact on violence derives not from the mediatized exaggeration of scenes of violence, as is commonly claimed, but in its emphasis on *happiness* … What incites real violence is less the avalanche of violent images as the difference between reality and that which is held up as a model, the breach that separates the demand to consume from its real costs. If it is true that television fabricates a happy violence—that is, a rapid, painless violence conceived so as to cause no obstacle to a happy ending—it is no less true that [post-Fordist] television is also the medium that confronts those most susceptible to violence with images of consumer happiness. (Lipovetsky, 2007, 185–186)

There has been ample theorization of the new global capitalism. But the perspectives, considerations and results of these theorizations take the First World as their orienting axis; they only consider the Third World to be *Spare-Part-Factory-Countries* that supply cheap labor and immigrants. Further, though their value judgments take categories like gender, class, and race into account, these are not considered to be desirable or important attributes, meaningful enough to justify a valid and autonomous discourse outside of their communities; they are conceded no right to universality.

We do not assert the right to universalize any discourse over others, and it remains crucial to underscore that it is impossible to do so. These subjects are not seen as active subjects of their own theorizations, since they are not granted the space nor the authority to speak or theorize about their own reality. In fact, those subjects who do speak are not listened to seriously. As Walter Mignolo writes,

> The power relation marked by colonial difference and established by the coloniality of power (that is, the discourse that justifies colonial difference) is what reveals that knowledge, like economics, is organized according to centers of power and subaltern regions. The trap is that the discourse of modernity created the illusion that knowledge is dis-embodied and de-localized, and that it is necessary for all parts of the planet to "ascend to" the epistemology of modernity. (Mignolo, 2003b, 2)

Third World subjects rarely escape victimizing or hierarchical visions, or those laden with *good* or foolish intentions. This is plainly seen in the theorizations on the "feminization of labor" as a synonym for precarity and as a clear and unequivocal feature of the great wave of female migration.[3]

Another biased way of reading Third World subjectivities is to stereotype them as suppliers of illegal goods, criminals, or potential criminals. These labels show only one side of the dyad of gore consumption: the supply side. Yet, if we follow the logic of the market and its law of supply and demand, we realize that the role of the consumer of illegal goods is made invisible. That side—the side of the consumer—is usually occupied by First World subjects.

Gore Consumption

This section will begin by looking more closely at the side of the gore consumer: a citizen with an average level of purchasing power who consumes for their own personal use and enjoys goods, products and services available on the gore market, i.e. drugs, prostitution, human organs, violence for intimidation purposes, contract killings, etc. The demand for all of these is founded on a specific geopolitical approach that views developing countries as manufacturing centers for gore merchandise meant to satisfy international recreational and practical demand. In this way, "international demand promotes an array of increasingly transnational criminal activities" (Curbet, 2007, 63).

These consumption practices are not new, since as Courtwright explains with reference to drugs: "the market in psychoactive products constitutes an essential element in the formation of the modern world; it is the external manifestation of mature capitalism's radical turn toward pleasure and emotional gratification to the detriment of the consumer's material needs" (Curbet, 2007, 67). As Misha Glenny puts it in *McMafia*:

> "No longer is it a sinful secret of the moneyed elite," reported *Time* in a July 1981 edition featuring a cocktail glass full of coke on the cover, "nor merely an elusive glitter of decadence in raffish society circles, as it seemed in decades past. No longer is it primarily an exotic and ballyhooed indulgence of high-gloss entrepreneurs, Hollywood types and high rollers ... [it is] the most conspicuous of consumptions, to be sniffed from the most chic of coffee tables ... Because it is such an emblem of wealth and status, coke is the drug of choice for perhaps millions of solid, conventional, and often upwardly mobile citizens. (Glenny, 2008, 245)

What is new about these consumption practices is, on the one hand, the way they have intensified and become so artificially naturalized[4] as to be openly demanded by society; on the other hand, the fact that these practices have escaped moral judgment and are now interpreted as relevant according to the criteria of economic theory. As the previous citation demonstrates, drug consumption is no longer understood as a *luxury*; so, following economic logic, what arises is "big growth ... in markets where demand is growing even faster than incomes as we become more and more prosperous" (Coyle, 2004, 7).

The introduction of hedonistic consumption as a mass phenomenon has overdeveloped one part of our lives: the mentality of the individual who does well at everything and uses their massive consumption to display their social success and status. This idea has been imported to places where things cannot be bought safely, but rather only through the force of violence; thus, what is created is a dissonant reality where the logic of consumption fuels the hope that one "might one day have such luxury, even in the outskirts" (Saviano, 2008, 90).

This unequal interaction between worlds (the economically powerful and those economically deprived on the periphery) has caused economically-deprived countries to import this First World discourse with its dizzying speed, its need for advancement, and its race toward "progress." These countries have created undesirable strategies—that is thanato-strategies[5] or gore practices—in order to enter the global consumption race, retrofitting the logic of consumption, and introducing a gore sovereignty parallel to the state. As Achille Mbembe has explained:

> When resources are put into circulation, the consequence is a disconnection between people and things that is more marked than it was in the past, the value of things generally surpassing that of people. This is one of the reasons why the resulting forms of violence have as their chief goal the physical destruction of people, including massacres of civilians, genocides, and various kinds of killing, and the primary exploitation of things. These forms of violence, of which war is only one aspect, contribute to the establishment of sovereignty outside the state, and are based on a confusion between power and fact, between public affairs and private government. (Mbembe, "At the Edge of the World," 260)

The use of violence as an everyday, guilt-free practice means that this extra-state sovereignty complicates the relation between violence and the economy. It also reveals the limitations of existing theorizations of the real function of violence in the contemporary world, since it leads to "crime [being] vindicated as a normal form of life [in which many people] cannot *live like everyone*" (Lipovetsky, 2007, 184–185). This fluid series of conditions extends both the scope and the consequences of violence, naturalizing them, blurring the lines between the illegal economy—which creates an alternative state rooted in violence—and the legal economy, since both provide support for the society of hyperconsumption. Contemporary reality cannot be understood or described in all its complexity without considering violence and consumption as its central axes.

Though there is a wide and diverse variety of theorizations of contemporary capitalism, it is notable that the majority of them focus on the close ties between pleasure and hyperconsumerist consciousness. In other words, the production and acquisition of pleasure (at all levels) is both the engine and the transformative material of desire and lack of capital. An example of this is the notion of *pharmacopornographic* capitalism proposed by Paul B. Preciado:

> We are being confronted with a new kind of hot, psychotropic, punk capitalism … Our world economy is dependent on the production and circulation of hundreds of tons of synthetic steroids and technically transformed organs, fluids, cells (techno-blood, techno-sperm, techno-ovum), on the global diffusion of a flood of pornographic images, on the elaboration and distribution of new varieties of legal and illegal synthetic

psychotropic drugs (e.g., bromazepam, Special K, Viagra, speed, crystal, Prozac, ecstasy, poppers, heroin), on the flood of signs and circuits of the digital transmission of information, on the extension of a form of diffuse urban architecture to the entire planet in which megacities of misery are knotted into high concentrations of sex-capital … These are just some snapshots of a postindustrial, global, and mediatic regime that, from here on, I will call *pharmacopornographic*. (Preciado, 33)

Preciado is aware of the somatic and epistemological change that this new form of capitalism brings with it. This change can be understood as displacing the categories of humanism with hedonistic ones that entail an absolute change in the conception and apprehension of reality.

If consumer needs become the sole believable basis for interpreting reality and if interaction and socialization between people is confined to the realm of consumption, this means that even those individuals who inhabit "the poorest peripheral neighborhoods participate in the individualist and consumerist values of the middle classes, in their preoccupation with personality and individual self-realization" (Lipovetsky, 2007, 182–183). Humanism is displaced as the central epistemology of modernity in favor of a consumerist hedonism that—with its focus on producing commodities capable of satisfying hedonistic urges—obscures a process of violence, blood, and death.

Thus, Preciado's vision of pharmacopornographic capitalism explains a growing problem in contemporary societies ruled by consumerist hedonism that is intimately tied to micro-surveillance typical of control-oriented societies. At the same time, Preciado theorizes economically hyper-marginalized communities whose subjects participate *corporeally* in the representation of peripheral capitalist subjectivities. Nevertheless, we have to analyze these capitalist and pharmacopornographic subjectivities within the context of the gore economy, a context as yet unexamined in contemporary conceptual discourses. These discourses have neglected the category of violence, which appears at all stages of the pharmacopornographic process that Preciado describes, since violence underlies the entire development of the system and is specifically linked to the use of drugs and the pursuit of sexual pleasure. We should not ignore the fact that both of these phenomena are linked to organized crime and to violence as a tool for the production and management of their commodities and are thus primarily situated in the realm of the underground economy.

We therefore identify a fundamental connection between Preciado's *pharmacopornographic capitalism* and this book's argument about *gore capitalism*. This connection is based on our thesis that the production, trafficking and distribution of legal and illegal drugs are at the core of contemporary capitalism.

Preciado argues that this new capitalist paradigm can be used to analyze the *entire planet*, in other words, it is also applicable for peripheral subjects, for the Others. But these subjects routinely show up in discourse as curiosities or sources of color and/or marginality, not as embodied subjects. This does not mean that peripheral, non-hegemonic and largely Third World subjects lack the capacity to produce their own discourses; as we will attempt to show, these subjects construct practices that both uphold and resist the market's imperatives. Nonetheless, it is assumed that they are "not theoretical enough, because they are usually accessible to the reader and deal with uncomfortable, violent and non-abstract realities of oppression, race and class" (Moraga & Anzaldúa, 1983, 187).

The discourse of the new pharmacopornographic capitalism becomes interesting and daring in its consideration of the body as an eternally desirous, stimulated, interconnected and medicated apparatus. Nonetheless, this investigation into the body as a desirous apparatus does not have a clear relationship with *real bodies*, which perish from things that are *more real* than medications. Bodies are annihilated in gruesome and dramatic ways in economic and armed conflicts; bodies are depleted by work; bodies are commodities that are continually incapable of managing their own autonomy, because they were denied that autonomy at birth or because it has been robbed from them. Therefore, though we consider pharmacopornographic capitalism to be one of the conceptual tools necessary to explain the economic transformation of reality, in our work we look for ways to link it with gore capitalism in an attempt to clarify the scope of the practices and consequences of the contemporary world's voracious form of capitalism over the long term.

Further theorizations of capitalism are essential; these new theorizations expose the large gaps in knowledge that exist between the First and the Third Worlds. We think it crucial to have a steady flow of discourses analyzing the transformation of capitalism, and for each one of these currents to be allowed to overflow into others to power a g-local discursive turn, to allow all of us to perceive a variety of realities at one time. These multiple discourses would give rise to an aleph[6] that might be able to reveal the voracity of the current phase of capitalism. This aleph would forge a radical critique that could lead us first to think and, subsequently, to develop new forms of economic stewardship that turn away from speculation, accumulation, and bloodshed as driving economic forces.

The Formation of Gore Capitalism

It is practically impossible to create a genealogy of gore capitalism, framing specific events and exhaustively enumerating them, since one of the fundamental characteristics for the development and propagation of this type of capitalism has been its own spectralization. Gore capitalism has grown stronger because it has spread imperceptibly (and in many cases, it has been managed, protected, and demanded by the economic centers of world powers). It has been underestimated as something that is in the atmosphere but that lacks the effective force to develop on its own. Thus, over the course of a long process, the conditions have been created wherein *the creatures of the state*[7] and the economy threaten to devour the state.

Where everything seems to lie dormant, the force of capitalism has ramped up desire itself; the media and their propagation of consumerist desire work to catalyze it even further. As this acceleration intensifies, potential energy becomes kinetic energy in an enormous and unremitting process. Desire is crystallized in certain practices that become commodities; then subject-particles that once seemed harmless fit into place, embed themselves in us. Little by little, in a dispersed and erratic fashion, our tacit agreements around ethics or submission are destroyed. Brutal economic realities

and their circumstances mean that bodies, subjects, and flesh itself become centers, merchandise,
and exchange. Capital accumulation through dis-
turbance, reformulation, and infiltration of the
production process through necroempowerment.
Rupture. Disruption.

We can locate a crucial juncture for the development of gore capitalism in the great qualitative leap
brought on by the liberalization of markets from
1971 onward. In addition, the years from 1971 to
1973 witnessed the liberalization of the monetary
system—the origin of the great paradox implied by
the term spectralization. "All of this comes to a
head after 1989 with the fall of the Soviet bloc and
the end of the Cold War, which creates the conditions for a global commodity circuit and turns the
labor force into a commodity emigrating in all
directions" (Estévez & Taibo (2008), 54). The fall
of the Soviet bloc also leads to the triumphal inau-
guration of the *other economy*, the economy of
organized crime, no longer understood as a local
economic process but rather as any other transnational corporation, organized according to the
demands of the capitalist structure and the financial markets.

Another important consequence of the fall of
the USSR was the radicalization of capitalism, now
demagogically established as the only economic
system possible. Once capitalism becomes the sole

economic model, we can no longer speak of other possibilities for developing different economic projects, since the ones that exist are just variations of the same. There are three variations on the model: Anglo-Saxon, European, and Asian. At a fundamental level, all three use gore practices as economic engines, since gore capitalism cannot be reduced to illegality, but is simply crystallized and made evident in that realm. There is no room anymore for alternative economic ideologies; everything is reduced to profit, business and capital, nothing more.

This gore capitalism—characterized by its practices of explicit, conspicuous violence—also provides a name for a system that "allows 50,000 people to die every day, allows large multinational pharmaceutical companies to withhold assistance to combat huge pandemics and allows these extreme social inequities" (Estévez and Taibo, 2008).

This variation of capitalism is fed by rabid neoliberalism that reinforces its consequences, making them socially palpable; it forces people to feel the real impacts of this bitter form of neoliberalism. Gore capitalism derives from neoliberalism, yet it is not circumscribed or exhausted by it; rather it follows two separate paths. On the one hand it remains under control: even if illegal, it remains a full participant in capitalist logic, welcomed and patronized as a powerful investor by governments and multinationals that assist with money laundering and tax havens. On the other hand, it departs from the mandates of capitalism's hegemonic colonialist masters even as it remains closely linked to hyperconsumption.

Gore capitalism and its subjects have clear hierarchies—albeit distorted ones—since the most visible subjects are not always those that occupy the lowest rungs on the ladder. A further paradox is centered on endriago subjects, some of whom become charismatic subjects for the civil population, icons of adulation and respect.

Narcoculture and the New Criminal Class

In his book *Le bonheur paradoxal* [Paradoxical Happiness], Gilles Lipovetsky argues that poverty—understood discursively as a social class—has undergone a kind of devaluation. Given the exigencies of contemporary capitalism, this category no longer serves to unify a group of people in order to provide them with a sense of belonging, to grow together, or to foment activities that would lead to interpersonal connections and solidarity. Despite this, living through a process of social decomposition and disintegration imposed by hyperconsumerist discourse does not mean that these outcasts have no need for signposts of identity or belonging. One example of this fact is that the figure of the *heroic gangster* shows up repeatedly in depressed economic situations.

This iconization of various (primarily male) local criminals and the creation of a *pop culture* around organized crime cause both the underprivileged and society more broadly to ally their identities with them.

On the one hand, this phenomenon transcends economic law and leads to the creation of a *cultural stockpile* that bestows legitimacy through symbolic value on organized crime, thus giving rise to a narrative that allows it to intervene in social and ethical reality and to reconfigure it with popular support. As Guattari points out, subjectivity is created along with exterior processes and exceeds individuation, or more specifically:

> Subjectivity is not situated in the individual field, but in every process of social and material production. What one might say, using the language of computers, is that an individual always exists, but only as a terminal; this *individual terminal occupies the position of a consumer of subjectivity*. It consumes systems of representation, sensibility, and so on—which have nothing to do with natural, universal categories (Guattari & Rolnik, 45).

On the other hand, this glorification of criminal culture is established as a new market niche for production and consumption, spawning new fashions for the underprivileged classes with the subsequent need for international supply and demand. Examples of this can be found in multiple television series that revolve around the creation of crime heroes (e.g. *The Sopranos*) or videogames like *Grand Theft Auto* or, more recently, films like Guy Ritchie's *Rockanrolla* (2008). In this film, symptomatically, among other things, the archetype of the rock star (which since the 1960s has been the model to follow for urban teenagers worldwide looking for a desirable and glamorous identity) has been displaced by that of the mafioso, the new, true rock star of the twenty-first century. This displacement speaks to the process by which the entertainment-oriented mass media makes way for this new paradigm of identity among the privileged and First World classes.

> [T]he media tend[s] to acquire undue importance. They reinforce the state in its extended function. The function of these facilities, like workers on a machine for the formation of capitalist subjectivity, is to integrate human, infrahuman, and extrahuman factors, creating a real articulation between agencies as different as those at work in libidinal economy (such as family systems) and in semiotic productions (such as the media). (Guattari & Rolnik, 2008, 57)

The fashionability of the new-school mafioso (a more modern figure, operating without rules or borders, breaking with the ethical pacts of the old-school mafia) welcomes what is already happening throughout the Third World into the First World. The danger in all of this is that, through the artificial and playful naturalization of this archetype, the doors are opened to these subjectivities as something desirable; however, what is not shown are their dystopian consequences at the level of the real, off-screen and without that distance protecting the viewer from the consequences.

The glorification of the figure of the mafioso becomes a means of repeated and reciprocal reaffirmation by the masses, whether trhough consumption, imitation of mafia clothing styles or justification of the attitudes and violence that accompany this figure. This reificiation is inscribed within the logics of the production of capitalist subjectivities, since this system of production pre-forms (and in fact constitutes) contemporary subjectivity. Guattari and Rolnik argue as much:

> The capitalistic order produces modes of human relations even in their unconscious representations: the ways in which people work, are educated, love, have sex, and talk. And that's not all. It manufactures people's relations with production,

> nature, events, movement, the body, eating, the
> present, the past, and the future—in short, it
> manufactures people's relations with the world
> and with themselves. And we accept all this
> because we assume that this is 'the' world order,
> an order that cannot be touched without endan-
> gering the very idea of organized social life.
> (Guattari and Rolnik, 2008, 58)

This can be taken to be one of the fundamental
conditions for the heroification of the mafioso, the
criminal, the murderer (endriago subject); all of
them are now identified as winners according to
capitalist logic. At the same time, what is created
with these figures is an imaginary within which
popular interpretations legitimate and justify them
as models of *progress* and wealth dictated by hyperconsumption and the global market. This remains
the case even when their access to this model of
progress is achieved through alternative means,
founded in a categorical Machiavellianism that
holds that *the ends justify the means*.

Far from hiding their activities, the majority of
these charismatic endriago subjects broadcast them
far and wide, converting them into a model of
necroempowerment that, due to rising economic
precarity, has become desirable on a worldwide
level. In this way, we see the rise of a culture based
on the reification of crime.

Another example of this process is *narcoculture* (Resa, 2003)—the way of life forged and popularized by Mexican drug cartels and particularly visible in the northern part of Mexico. It features its own clothing styles, music (*narcocorridos*), a cinematic subgenre, consumption practices and a characteristic social status. This *narcoculture* is an example of the new reality *after* the dissolution of the established social classes (especially in Mexico, where the incipient middle class is already headed for extinction) and their reformulation into a new social class.

Thus, gore practice and their practitioners have created a new social class: the *global criminal class*. That is to say, these organizations have already moved far beyond the level of ethics—which would both limit and repudiate criminality; they have flipped ethics upside down, creating another kind of socialization, another *status*: that of respectability provided by money, no matter its provenance. This new structure has been adopted by the least privileged as a marker of identity and a sign of belonging. In the increasingly non-existent nation-states of the Third World, what has been established is a new nationalist culture based on criminality.

However, this reification of criminality in economically-depressed countries has not occurred arbitrarily; in many cases, endriago subjects and their cartels are assuming the role of the state. In the specific case of Mexico, these endriagos (many of whom come from campesino (peasant) classes) are taking on the responsibility of stimulating agricultural production. Logically, this assistance centers on drug production. Other functions of the state handled by the narcos include the construction of infrastructure like highways, schools, hospitals and even churches, since many of these subjects consider themselves to be pious Catholics.

There is no doubt that the Church and organized crime in Mexico, especially drug traffickers, maintain a very close relationship, since the narcos, at least until recent years, have largely come from rural areas where education is scarce and the Catholic religion has an overwhelming presence (see Resa 2003). Nonetheless, as the narco's Catholic faith has become intertwined with ritual practices characteristic of organized crime, both have begun to change.[8] There have even been cases of narcos who build churches or give sizable donations in exchange for priests to sprinkle holy water on drug shipments bound for the United States.

While the question of the countryside merits a more detailed discussion than we will offer here, we will still develop some brief reflections on this issue, since we see it as a central aspect in the rise of gore capitalism in the form of drug trafficking.

Campesinos have been the first to experience the clear effects of the radicalization of globalization in the countryside. Forced impoverishment, a lack of governmental assistance and the imposition of absurd taxes have obligated them to emigrate to large urban centers to become cheap labor. In an economic system based on existential and financial precarity, they have been displaced once again and have been left without land. This displacement, coupled with ever-more-terrifying drops in the price of labor, has left them in an intolerable position, without work and without opportunities.

Thus, for the least privileged, the logic of capitalism is entirely destructive. In this context, it is not surprising that campesinos would decide to cooperate with drug traffickers. Emigration to the United States, suicide[9] or collaboration with the drug cartels are among the few options left open under neoliberalism's ferocious logic.

It is an interesting fact that drug trafficking in Mexico is the product of a campesino struggle that became an urban guerrilla force, which in turn became organized crime and finally gore capitalists who have mutated into large-scale investors in the world economy.[10] In this way, they have reconfigured the very concept of social mobility.

We are not looking to praise endriago subjects, nor are we trying to elide the repression and terror they exercise through their violence on the civil population. Nonetheless, we thought it important to show the implicit complexity in the very particular reinterpretation of contemporary capitalism made by these subjects with their gore practices.

What we find in the contemporary world is the paradox of both uneven development and a calculated social homogenization offered by the path of consumerism; with this paradox, we attempt to contextualize the coexistence of extreme unequal development that occurs not only in distinct territories but also in poor sectors that have grown and overlapped in a First World that increasingly resembles the Third World. In this context, what arises is the need to investigate the circumstances and daily lives of these underprivileged subjects, lifeways that have been hidden by the contemporary hyperconsumerist framework.

Within this contemporary hyperconsumerist framework, we need to move beyond descriptions of it made by the middle classes, which have been fully integrated into the labor market. We need to ask what is happening to the other social strata, in particular those groups who have been affected by new levels of precarity and are falling into new forms of poverty?

When millions of people live below the poverty line or in extremely precarious economic conditions, the model of *perpetually deferred satisfaction* begins to show its limitations (Lipovetsky, 2007, 180–1).

The fact that the birth of gore capitalism finds its most visible and ferocious home in Third World countries with depressed economies follows more than merely economic logic. It also obeys a logic based on surreptitious insubordination and on a lack of any discourse that might impede action. It is well-known that when we lack the necessary information or when we lack concepts to articulate our condition—to explain ourselves to ourselves— there is a tendency to act without prior theorization. Action is impossible to stop when faced with a system of continual rejection and frustration, a system ruled by orders and counter-orders.

Given this system of orders and counter-orders (with its origins in colonial times)[11] under which individuals rarely have the opportunity to posit themselves as subjects with agency, it is not surprising that "testosterone-fueled, unemployed young men, who are often well armed" (Glenny, 41) would decide to join the mafia or to create their own mafias themselves. In this way, they are able to comply with the orders and directives of the heteropatriarchal and misogynist capitalism of the West, as it is only through this inherited discourse that they are able to feel legitimated and empowered.

Lydia Lunch says: *I sell frustration not relief* (Lunch, 2004). This proposition—which can be applied to the economic system of hyperconsumerist societies—illustrates one of the most important maxims undergirding capitalist logic. It offers a political characterization of frustration as one of the engines of capitalism (and by identifying it renders it public, connecting it to the global market as a source of capital). In addition, it shows us "the covert engines of capitalism of the twenty-first century," a twin achievement: "it is a marginal and hidden aspect of the contemporary cultural industry, but it is also a paradigm for all other types of post-Fordist production" (Preciado, 267).

This understanding of frustration as the engine of capitalism is directly connected to the construction of the subjectivity of individuals who make up mafia networks and the illegal economy. In what follows, we will present the case of narco subjectivity, without "opposing the relations of economic production to the relations of subjective production" (Guattari & Rolnik, 2006, 38).

The narco is glorified, and narcoculture grows because we live in a society in which individuals who want to become heroes find no ways to do so. If education, the law and the struggle for social justice cannot make a hero, what's left? Crime. The only area in which rural and urban heroism is possible. Here then is the foolproof formula for turning your child into a narco, a criminal, someone thirsty for more and more power.

From a very early age, grind up your kid's feelings, body and desires. Tell your kid that you know more about them than they do. Tell your kid that everything they do is "bad." (Do this as regularly as possible.) As you work to give form to a person marked by this sense of *incompleteness*, add machismo, classism, racism and misogyny into the mix. Do this until you have successfully created a person who is only "complete" when they cut others down. (Derision is the key ingredient in this traditional dish.)

Once your kid reaches puberty, increase the level of your familial authoritarianism. Use emotional blackmail or overt violence. Maintain a warlike familial environment. By this time, your kid will be looking for any way to stand out. You and your society must block any attempt to excel through education, love or work.

Bring the mixture to boil with *narcocorridos* and Hollywood movies. Add two grams of cocaine. Or bake it with marijuana or meth (sold without a prescription). On low heat, let your kid roam the streets. There your kid will find the nearest gang, cop, cartel, or army. Then he will have "respect." And he will take his revenge on you and on the entire society. For dessert, play the victim and ask yourself why there are such heartless people in the world when you yourself are so sweet. (Yépez, 2008)

Heriberto Yépez's irony speaks to the processes behind the creation of narco subjectivity, based as it is on continual lack and frustration, the axes of the capitalist system. At the same time, he makes us aware of the responsibility each one of us bears within this system.

By exposing and despectralizing everyday reality, Yépez speaks to the need for us all, as individuals and collectively, to take notice of what is happening in this system whose primary aim is to sell us frustration, not relief. Recognizing this system for what it is can lead us to act in critical and self-aware ways in relation to our (unalienated) labor and practices within the system of gore production.

Uneven Development of History and Gore Capitalism

In her call for a deontological ethics (made via an adaptation of the Kantian categorical imperative), Adela Cortina writes: "The first commandment is to do no harm." That said, we turn to an analysis of the constant tendency to forget that History— or least historical discourses—is grounded in uneven development.

If we fail to consider History's uneven development, we quickly forget that certain concepts of humanism, ethics and other Western discourses— which are thought to be unquestionable, desirable, and morally acceptable in the First World—lack that status in other contexts and political geographies. This means that in other societies (with distinct histories of development and distinct conceptual frames) these categories are considered empty, abstract, and removed from everyday realities.

We should not elide the fact that the establishment of concepts like *equality, liberty, and fraternity* emerged during a specific historical context in a specific culture. And yet these concepts are exported into other cultures (or there is an attempt to do so) and subsequently these cultures are asked to conform to a homogeneous code of conduct based on the thought and practices of the West.[12]

Nor should we naturalize or erase the fact that the acceptance and adoption of these concepts in the West has not always been consensual—that these concepts are not inherent but the results of a process of *education* and legitimation enacted through performative utterances and metaphors that produce that with which they purport to describe. Namely, "that which has been known since the days of Cicero as *humanism* is in the narrowest and widest sense a consequence of literacy" (Sloterdijk, 2009, 12).

We cannot expect the same results from the same variable in disparate contexts. We must break with the "solipsistic delusion that [we] live in a history solely of [our] own making" (Davis, 2002, 2). To do so, we need geopolitically situated forms of knowledge.

All of this is relevant to understand the brutal effects of extreme violence on us. The interesting thing is not that this violence affects us in a clear and unequivocal manner, but rather that it surprises us—a fact that should alert us that our inattention to the Other in our theorizations is exacting a price. We are unable to confront other dynamics because we are ignorant of them and because our efforts are wedded to the project of legitimating the West as the only reality and possibility.

Namely, while the West lives under a *pharmaco-pornographic and/or biopolitical* capitalism of microcellular surveillance, immersed in a high-tech and high-speed hypermodernity, subjects in other spaces live, theorize, and act based on their own realities. These realities are not disconnected from a West that they are in fact increasingly influencing and reconfiguring; when we get news of these other realities, they explode in our faces and we are horrified.

It is as if we lived in interconnected *wormholes*, a metaphor that interconnects space and time despite them being out of sync: a *patchwork* of Histories in which temporal tectonic plates interlock and crash against one another in the context of uneven development.

In light of this, we can argue that Cortina's words—and her deontological maxim, *Do No Harm*—are embedded in the reasoning and the context of a First World reality governed (or which at least boasts of being governed) by a rule of law that enforces compliance with ethical norms. Notwithstanding this fact, we should remember that: "For the last five centuries, the (relative) prosperity and peace of the 'civilized' West was attained through the export of ruthless violence and destruction into the 'barbarian' Outside: the long story from the conquest of America to the slaughter in Congo" (Žižek, 2002, 6).

Cortina's maxim is reformulated and overturned by the realities of gore capitalism, which are not limited to the Third World but rather are rapidly expanding with globalization and the unification of world capital across the entire planet. Cortina's affirmation is relativized and brazenly questioned: if the first commandment (for the West) is *Do No Harm*, the response from the deprived is a question: *Do No Harm?* and an affirmation: *Receive no more harm*, or *Participate in harm as agents and no longer (only) as victims*. This affirmation is posited as another—an Other's—form of empowerment (inconceivable from the viewpoint of Western ethics).

In this sense, Roberto Saviano, reflecting on the breach between ethical judgments and actions, writes: "For some reason one stupidly thinks a criminal act has to be more thought out, more deliberate than an innocuous one. But there's really no difference. Actions know an elasticity that ethical judgments ignore" (Saviano, 2008, 14). The furious speed of capitalism's transfiguration into gore has subverted the ethical agreements that have governed Western humanism until now. This hardcore version of capitalism has blasted them apart and projected them far outside of its own limits.

Ethics have become an accessory in this hyperconsumerist, ultracapitalist world, since they are perceived as "the limit of the loser, the protection of the defeated, the moral justification for those who haven't managed to gamble everything and win it all" (Saviano, 2008, 112). The categorical imperative has been displaced by the economic imperative.

In this context of systematic exclusion and uneven development, the concept of justice has also been reinterpreted. First, it has been separated from the concept of law. For endriago subjects in gore capitalism the terms are not equivalent, since the law has pre-established codes that do not permit criminal practices. Justice as an abstract concept allows greater malleability around the interpretation of non-stigmatized acts of extreme violence, since for these subjects justice only has meaning in concrete circumstances. Thus a sort of alternative axiology arises, one approving of all those methods and actions used by gore capitalism as *just*, because its notion of justice is focused on the pursuit of two basic goals: wealth accumulation and victory over all competitors.

We can thus speak of uneven development in the pertinence and applicability of humanist discourse in territories decontextualized from it. In the case of the Third World we can say: "[its] developments over the long term, its rapid deviations and temporalities [and effects] of long duration are not necessarily separate, nor simply overlapping. Some fit inside of others, some stand in for others; at times some cancel others out, while at other times some multiply the effects of others" (Mezzadra, 2008, 168).

With the previous quote, we seek to show that the appropriations and repercussions of humanist discourse in the Third World are diverse, affecting it in a multi-vectored and non-hegemonic fashion. We do not deny the impact of humanist discourse on the actions of endriago subjects, or claim that the Third World is entirely removed from it; we merely affirm that its applicability and repercussions are in a state of total becoming and of constant reinterpretation. Ethics in the Third World, more than a process, are an *in situ* action.

Such reinterpretations will be incomprehensible if our efforts at understanding remain tied to a Western and hierarchical posture that only allows us to perceive them with an exoticizing lens. This approach can lead only to a total rejection, whereby we denigrate and underestimate these practices by labeling them as practices common in underdeveloped and barbaric cultures. On the other hand, acritical glorification of difference—a romanticization that treats these practices as emancipatory responses to First World dynamics—ignores their drawbacks and all that is problematic about them and remains blind to their inflection points.

An example of this romanticization—although not an acritical one—is Negri and Cocco's defense of the Third World as "a laboratory for new experiments in the relations between governments and social movements" (Negri and Cocco, 2007, 3). These theorists claim that Third World subjects— whether they live in so-called Third World countries, on the borders of the First World or in the socially-peripheral spaces inside the First World— are the driving force for reorienting the political management of the state's governmentality:

the insurrection in the French banlieues or the Brazilian favelas, the flight from the countryside, are already sketching radically open and new horizons: these insurrections show us that the

inhabitants of the countryside are the raw material, the flesh of the multitude from which the
globalized world is made. (Negri and Cocco,
2007, 1)

But their idealizing enthusiasm does not allow
them to show us the hidden and complex side of
the actions undertaken by these (masculine)
peripheral subjects. They do not analyze the
impact these practices have on the normalization
of dystopian and criminal practices since they leave
out an important sector of insurrectionist subjects
created and nurtured by globalization: criminal
subjects, the endriagos of gore capitalism.

Consequently, it is crucial to develop another
line of interpretation to understand the destruction
of ethical norms by endriago subjects, since they
toe the line of the most radical dictates of the market. We are forced to leave behind the dichotomy of
good versus evil—so familiar to criticism—even
when it is expressed in hyper-specialized and
grandiose terms. We must learn to speak about
things in other ways, as subjects divorced from
Manichean logic, without falling into facile celebra-
tions of a "light" Third-Worldism that "combine[s]
the most disparate and passing fads, the most contradictory inspirations" (Finkielraut, 1995, 111).

We know that every culture justifies itself and its
practices according to its own needs and internal

contexts. But this does not mean that the modes of empowerment that result should be accepted at any price, especially if they have been achieved by dystopian means. Nor does it mean that *everything is cultural and therefore all cultures are equally legitimate*, since speaking of the concept of culture as universal erases the specificity of cultures as well as their forms of agency. For this reason, we cannot indiscriminately employ the terms *culture* and *multiculturalism* to refer to a hyperconsumerist social formation that understands difference not as a right to be defended but as a synonym for an *ample range of consumer options*.

We wish to make it clear that—though perhaps difficult to detect at first glance—humanism has a complex, important, and undeniable role in the logic of gore. The foundation of gore is humanism itself, and their relationship makes the concept of gore relevant for discussions of contemporary capitalism. This is not a linear or singular relationship, but rather gore capitalism participates in the discourse of humanism even as it subverts it or dissents from it, for the discourse of humanism is not applicable to the everyday economic and political conditions of the Third World,[13] given that "neoliberalism has no model for social integration" (Negri and Cocco, 2007, 2).

Nonetheless, the actions of endriago subjects participate in humanist discourse, and move beyond it by means of a new syncretism they forge from the social values of humanism, religion, and the dictates of the economy. This syncretism disrupts the position of parodic subalternity that has historically been assigned to them, a process that has degraded them to the point of "turn[ing] into a subject of pride what they had been taught to be ashamed of" (Finkielkraut, 1995, 68). Therefore, they seek their dignity and their affirmation of identity (both aspirations central to humanism) by means of a suicidal logic. These subjects will not die or kill for religion or in the name of a political cause but rather for money and power.

If these subjects entirely refused to participate in humanist discourse, there would be no way to create bridges between these worlds; we would be speaking of parallel but utterly disconnected worlds, utterly incomparable, worlds. Above all this would deny the possibility of discussing the relationship between them, of the ways they reciprocally judge and affect one another. This is a possibility we must retain in contemporary post-Fordist conditions where discourses are indeed comparable by means of their shared consumerist roots—conditions in which what once made humanist discourse now makes the discourse of the new hyperconsumerist capitalism. "Now even the least privileged want access to the emblematic symbols of the society of hyperconsumption, and they give every sign of individualist aspirations and behaviors—even if they are simply following the fashion" (Lipovetsky, 2007, 183).

Thus, humanist discourse has lost ground as hyperconsumerist discourse has become central to interpreting—and legitimating—the action of endriago subjects. It is crucial to add that as of now we have no way of knowing if these actions might give rise to a new equilibrium, an equilibrium that is inconceivable in the present moment.

If we analyze the actions of endriago subjects from an unequivocal moral perspective, we are only able to judge or condemn them, preventing us from constructing alternatives to becoming-gore. In the context of a concrete daily reality that transforms itself at incalculable speeds—and outstrips ethical rubrics in the process—a purely moral discourse leads us to simplify endriago actions, labeling them according to outdated parameters. For this reason, we should be wary of the temptation to other them, by creating interpretive discourses for these subjectivities that appeal to "the sociology of poverty or a metaphysics of the ghetto" (Saviano, 2008, 82), a simplistic reduction that renders them irreversible phenomena, confined to the margins in terms of human activities and possible thinking.

Instead of simplifying these subjectivities, we should think through them in their necropolitical and thanatophilic relations. We understand necropolitics to be the opposite of biopolitics. As for thanatophilia, we can say that it is historically inscribed in the roots of the "civilized" First World as much as in the de-realized Third World, and that it continues today as a common and growing practice, a way to train the mind for combat and warfare. For, in the First World as in the Third, "once we have committed the first murder and we are immersed in the pool of blood, the only way out is forward; going backward has no meaning, for if we retreat how can we explain what we have done?"[14] It is precisely here, in the break from humanist norms, that the actions of Third World endriago subjects and those of First World soldiers become connected, subsumed within the logics of hyperconsumerist society.

Distant though these actions may seem, they are closer to our daily reality than we like to admit, since:

> Consumerist pressures and attitudes do not stop at the borders of poverty; today they extend to all social levels, including those who depend on social security. On the one hand, post-Fordism is a tremendous machine socializing us into consumption; on the other, it disorganizes the behavior of entire categories of the population who find themselves unable to adapt to poverty

and to resist the temptations of the market. (Lipovetsky, 2007, 185)

In these circumstances, it is not surprising that endriago subjects employ gore practices to comply with consumerist demands, since these practices counteract feelings of failure and fault brought on by their reality. This is because

Material poverty is lived as a lack of autonomy and a lack of access to one's own projects, as the obsession with survival, as the feeling of failure and social collapse. In consumer societies, precarity intensifies psychological troubles, the conviction that one has failed at life. For those classes of people who are socialized by work and who enjoy a certain social mobility, properly material frustrations tend to diminish. Yet among the *underdogs* frustrations get worse and lead to the conviction that they are leading a life that *is not a life*. This is the violence of the civilization of happiness, its new ordeal. (Lipovetsky, 2007, 190)

Returning to our claim about history's uneven development, we would add that these actions that break so atrociously with humanist discourse do not find their genealogy in endriago subjectivity; rather, they expose the break with humanist norms that occurred long before the appearance of gore subjectivity. The roots of this epistemic break are situated in the First World's historical neglect and abusive use of the Third World. Necropolitics is re-positioned as a central motor of the management and application of economic and social policies in North-South relations.

Becoming-Endriago: Gore Capitalism's New Subjects

One would expect a gore capitalist society to have both an impact on and real consequences in the lives of its constituent subjects. This external and internal impact creates an interwoven, nearly irresolvable, controversy about whether social phenomena pre-form subjects and their behaviors—though subject formation is not an attempt at naturalizing or essentializing—or whether the subjects' bodies and actions create certain phenomena in reality. Put another way, the question becomes whether social reality has found its own agency, whether it has become a flexible, fluid structure, one that has an outward appearance that is sufficiently innocuous so as to infiltrate subject's bodies and reality itself on a massive scale. What is created is a two-fold structure that, on the one hand, acts from the inside-outside of the subject and has effects on reality and, on the other hand, is influenced by this reality and thus created as a subject. This structure is impossible to decipher at first glance, as it combines the production of new subjects and hyperconsumerist demands, instituting a continual feedback loop between internality and externality.

By the end of the nineteenth century, Nietzsche was already looking for the barbarians of the twentieth century. He imagined these subjects as "wild beasts, untamed, ferocious, but *fully alive*" (Berman, 2001, 208). Nietzche's *new men* were grounded in a pre-Christian pride, *blond beasts*[15] capable of returning home after "orgies of murder, arson, rape, torture, jubilant and at peace with themselves" (Berman, 2001, 208). Nietzsche never imagined that his characterization of the *blond beast* would be incarnated and brought to bear by mostly non-white and non-First World subjects. These subjects are bringing about the *rebarbarization of the world* that Nietzsche so fondly hoped for, at the same time as they deal a brutal blow to any romanticized image of the barbarian. These *barbarians*, who in all probability have not read Nietzsche, fulfill his ideas and respond to his question about where they can be found. These new barbarians tell us, with Nietzsche: "If you look too long into the abyss, the abyss will look back into you" (Berman, 2001, 208).

It is necessary to move beyond the exoticizing idyll, to leave behind "conceptualizations and compositions that oscillate between the extremes of victimhood and heroism, sympathy and glorification" (Mezzadra, et al., 2008, 239). We should stop using the concept of *marginalized subjects* under the cover of contemporary political correctness, for this contributes to a nebulous generalization that prevents us from delving deeper into these subjectivities in order to take full stock of them in their position within the contemporary economic system. It is crucial to resist both the temptation to exoticize and intellectual indolence.

We are faced with a capitalism that simultaneously produces capital and destroys bodies, a capitalism founded on the speculation of bodies-as-commodities, based on "minimum investment [the use of violence and force], direct sales of the product in real time in a unique fashion, the production of instant satisfaction for the consumer" (Preciado, 2013, 39). The production of dead, mutilated, brutalized bodies becomes a kind of commodity that maintains and *justifies itself* according to the supply-and-demand logics of the new capitalism.

Murder is now conceived of as a transaction, extreme violence as a legitimate tool, torture as an ultra-profitable exercise and display of power. What was once understood as the *global underworld* has taken a leap forward and has now risen to the surface. Gore capitalism has infiltrated our lives; our very roles as consumers/spectators guarantee that we cannot remove ourselves from this fact. Much of our daily life is now rooted in organized crime. Gore can no longer be reduced to a film genre or to the pages of tabloids or sensationalist newspapers. Gore is our reality now.

As an example, take the new tendency to invest in drugs instead of in the stock market—a tendency apparent not only among a petite-bourgeoisie loyal to neoliberal principles but also among pensioners, workers, and small businesspeople, who:

> … hand over money to agents, who then invest it in drug lots. If you invested your pension of 600 euros in cocaine, you'd double your money in a month … The profit far outweighed the risk, especially compared with what one would have made in bank interest. (Saviano, 2008, 52)

A further example demonstrates how criminal practices have become interwoven in our everyday social lives and how the least likely subjects have come to participate in the criminal system:

> The lower-middle class is the perfect fit for an informal and hyperliberal distribution system. A friendly exchange, more like a Tupperware party, far removed from any criminal structures. Ideal for eliminating excessive moral responsibility. No

pusher in a silk acetate tracksuit planted for days on end in the corner of the marketplace, protected by lookouts. Nothing but the products and the money, just enough space for commercial exchange. (Saviano, 2008, 67)

These examples prompt us to inquire into the process by which one becomes an endriago subject. We must consider how a subject decides to re-appropriate reality and to re-form it in ways unimagined within any conceptual framework, to leave behind the original Aristotelian presuppositions that ground Western thought, to exile oneself from postmodern networks, and to seek self-legitimation in criminal structures and drug cartels as a way to write oneself into the narration of history's transformation as an active agent.

Jean Baudrillard speaks of what he calls the "revenge of the mirror people," writing

Here begins the great revenge of otherness, of all the forms which, subtly or violently deprived of their singularity, henceforth pose an insoluble problem for the social order, and also for the political and biological orders … But a being […] will one day rebel, and then our whole system of representation and values is destined to perish in that revolt. This slavery of the same, the slavery of resemblance, will one day be smashed by the violent resurgence of otherness. We dreamed of passing through the looking-glass, but it is the mirror peoples themselves who will burst in upon our world. And this time will not be defeated. (Baudrillard, 1996, 149)

In Baudrillard's words, we find a valid explanation to describe the rise of endriago subjects, as well as their current role in the world.

All That Is Solid Is Built On Blood

By what process does the real re-establish its irrefutable certitude and become a cog in the gears of gore capitalism? How has the worsening situation brought us to the re-affirmation of reality after so much virtual technology and so much theorizing about simulacra? Why do we require flesh, blood, and dismemberment to make reality true again? What demands have the world's economic powers made on the Third World? Did those powers expect the response to be blunt and violent? Can we speak today, beyond the biopolitical subject, of endriago subjects? As axes and actors of the new capitalism, endriago subjects replace the Marxist dictum, *All that is solid melts into air* with *All that is solid is built on blood*.

Gore capitalism is the result of endriago subjects' active, violent, and irreversible participation in the globalized market, hyperconsumption, and border territories. A historical pivot, a dystopian portrait. A paradox in the purest state. A problem that has become a key part of the contemporary world and which threatens to annihilate us. Surplus value and carnage. Endriagos as the new subjects of gore capitalism.

Now is the time to analyze gore capitalism as the adverse consequence of deregulated capitalist production, the violent collision and breakdown of layers of reality. As if reality had folded in on itself and we were now living in a discursive multi-reality whose only constants are the increasing wealth of the few and the bloodshed of the majority.

The world-wide spread of violence is one of the many dystopian elements of the globalizing project. This globalization, connected to the rise of endriago subjects, reveals both the raw truth of this project, the "absolutely specific fact of the necessary growth of world markets" (Negri, 2008, 53), and the very rigorous way in which endriago subjects mold themselves to the demands of the ultraliberal economy.

The economic and epistemological monopoly that grounds ultraliberal ideology has displaced all other ideologies of meaningful and active resistance. Nonetheless, this has been made possible by the disengagement and the nihilistic attitude of the New Left, converting it into a partner to neo-conservative and ultracapitalist neoliberalism. The left needs to make alliances with a wide array of social movements. Besides examining its own theoretical motivations, it needs to map out the practical activities that might reshape it into a school of thought that grounds resistance in the specific context of the problems that develop in our contemporary societies.

Because all marginalized (and non-marginalized) subjects who have been affected by the demands of hyperconsumerism are unrepresented in resistance discourses, they have the chance to become endriagos. For endriagos, their ability to represent themselves is based on their purchasing power and on their reshaping of the concept of resistance through dystopian actions. Thus, the endriagos attempt to define themselves from a sector that historically had been off limits and prohibited: crime.

If we examine the drug trade, we see that it is another way to deploy the globalizing catchphrase *delocalization*, by practicing a sort of *inverse delocalization* as it transgresses borders[16] to move its products and sell them in a flourishing and affluent market that has been demanding them for decades, in ever-increasing quantities. In this way, the trade in drugs fulfills the fundamental maxim of capitalism: have something to sell to someone who wants to buy it and thus make a profit.

The becoming-endriago can be understood as one more—very predictable—result of the contemporary economic process, which is known in its social incarnation as hyperconsumerism.

Definition and Characteristics of Endriago Subjects

We take the term *endriago* from medieval literature, specifically the book *Amadís de Gaula* [*Amadis of Gaul*].[17] We do so in alignment with Mary Louise Pratt's argument that the contemporary world is governed by *the return of the monsters* (Pratt, 2002, 1). The endriago is a literary character, a monster, a cross between a man, a hydra and a dragon. It is noted for its large stature, agility and beastliness; it is one of the enemies that Amadis of Gaul is forced to confront.[18] In the book, it is described as being endowed with defensive and offensive elements sufficient to provoke fear in any adversary. Its fierceness is so storied that the island where it lives is described as uninhabited, a kind of earthly hell which knights whose heroism borders on madness can enter. The descriptions of this island closely resemble contemporary border zones.[19]

We are making an analogy between the literary figure of the endriago—who belongs to the realm of the Others, the unacceptable and the enemy— and those people who this book has identified as the new ultraviolent, destructive subjects of gore capitalism: *endriago subjects.*

Endriago subjects have arisen out of a specific context: post-Fordism. This provides the evidence and a basic genealogy to explain the connection between poverty and violence, between the birth of endriago subjects and gore capitalism.

The everyday context of these subjects is "the very real juxtaposition of the proliferation of merchandise and exclusion from consumption; they are concurrent with the combination of a growing number of needs with the growing lack of almost basic resources for an important part of the population" (Lipovetsky, 2007, 181). This is in addition to the fact that:

> While some are immersed in an atmosphere of runaway consumption, others have seen the degradation of their quality of life, unending deprivations in the most essential sectors of the budget, absolute exhaustion with the hell they inhabit every day, the humiliation of being assisted by social security. If there is a nightmare of hyperconsumption, it is not visible in the *rise of insignificance* or in the insatiable thirst for commercial purchases: it is to be found in the degradation of material conditions, in the despondency caused by restrictions, the barest levels of consumption despite the daily, constant

bombardment of colorful temptations. Hell is not an endless spiral of consumption; it is the underconsumption of the vulnerable populations living in the heart of a hyperconsumerist society. (Lipovetsky, 2007, 181)

Hence, endriago subjects decide to utilize violence as a tool for empowerment and capital acquisition. Due to a number of factors—a few of which we will enumerate here—the use of direct violence is more and more popular among powerless populations. In many cases, it is seen as a response to the fear of demasculinization that haunts many men as a consequence of rising workplace precarity and their own subsequent inability to legitimately take on the role of male provider. On one hand, the poor no longer belong to a single social class; they no longer have a category or condition that includes them all. As Lipovetsky writes, "The mass poverty and defenselessness that exist in our societies bring about unfamiliar features" (182). This situation gives rise to features like the repudiation or derealization of the individual. A type of discursive abrogation that impacts any sense of meaning or possibility of belonging.

On the other hand, we are faced with the fact that "small crimes, theft and quick fixes as easy ways to get money and to participate in the dominant lifestyles that the media bombard us with"

(Lipovetsky, 2007, 184). What results is an epistemological change in the conception of violence, since it is perceived as a tool for personal self-affirmation and simultaneously as a means of subsistence.

In addition to the two factors mentioned previously, we can add that marginalized people also want to (have to) be consumers, since they seek a form of socialization/competition through consumption. "In current conditions, consumption constructs a large part of identity: when other means of recognition fail, making a buck and consumption prevail as foremost objectives" (Lipovetsky, 2007, 183).

It should be spelled out that it is not just the use of violence that is popularized, but also its consumption. In this way, violence is converted not only into a tool, but also into merchandise that is directed at a variety of market niches; one example is the marketing of *decorative violence* to the middle classes and privileged sectors. What this means is that no sector or market niche escapes the violence, whether it is presented as a merchandise supplying symbolic value or as a tool for dystopian empowerment.

In the case of the second, endriago subjects themselves expose the flipside of the consumption of violence, narrowing the distance between the power of consumption and the purchasing power obtained through the use of violence. Everything is brought together by consumption, as it is reinterpreted as a reaffirmation of identity, as triumph through purchasing and the reaffirmation of a status that is no longer social but individual. Thus we can say that:

> Mediator of *the true life*, consumption holds itself out as something that allows one to break free from social denigration and one's own negative self-image. The obsession with consumption— visible today even in marginalized populations— makes clear not just the unprecedented power of the commodification of lifestyles, but also the extraordinary intensity of frustrations vis-à-vis dominant lifestyles. In addition, there is an increased demand for consideration and respect, typical of an expressive individualism fostered by post-Fordism: the individual is more and more concerned with not feeling diminished, with their own wounded sense of dignity. (Lipovetsky, 2007, 183)

All of this elucidates more about the origins of the contradictions that have brought us to gore capitalism. Gore capitalism finds itself strengthened by the fact that:

> [o]n the one hand, young people in the peripheral neighborhoods of large cities internalize consumerist norms and values on a massive scale. On the other hand, poverty and precarious lives

prevent them from fully participating in consumption activities and in commercial entertainment. A slew of feelings of frustration and exclusion emerge out of this contradiction, along with criminal behaviors. (Lipovetsky, 2007, 183)

In terms of the identity characteristics of the endriago subject, they are "anomolous and transgressive, combining a mentality of lack (poverty, failure, dissatisfaction) with a mentality of excess, frustration, and heroification, a drive to hate and a utilitarian strategy" (Lipovetsky, 2007, 189). Endriago subjectivity:

… apparently does not coincide with the individualism of the victors, those with sufficient resources to be independent, but neither is it reducible to a negative or subjected individualism. The latter is manifested as victimhood, while the savage individualism [of the endriago subject] looks for illegitimate modes of action and self-affirmation to exorcize the image and condition of victimhood. One appeals to compassion or solidarity, while the other triggers calls for order and repression. Even in areas of social invalidation, there is a certain individualist competition, rife with brutal activism, defiance and self-endangerment that is far beyond the position of *individual by default*. (Lipovetsky, 2007, 189)

Using extreme violence, endriago subjects create a lifestyle, work, socialization, and culture. They remake work culture into a kind of dystopian Protestantism, in which work and life are fused together. Nevertheless, the endriagos reinterpret the notion of work and the practice of work, completely replacing the deity of Protestantism with money.

Endriagos also break with a logic of the world of work that is essentially prohibitive and rational, catapulting us into a new state in which work is reinterpreted and is comparable with violence, showing us an "excess [that] manifests itself in so far as violence wins over reason" (Bataille, 1986, 41).

Finally, we understand endriago subjects as a grouping of individuals defined by a capitalistic subjectivity filtered through increasingly precarious global economic conditions. Endriagos are also defined by a subjective agency based on ultraviolent practices that are able to reflect—in a self-referential way and from the borders—"the systems of direct connections between the great engines of production, the great machines of social control and the psychic agencies that define the way of perceiving the world" (Guattari & Rolnik, 2008, 37). In addition, they show us that "bodies embedded in a social process such as the circulation of variable capital are never to be construed as docile or passive" (Harvey, 2000, 117).

3

The New Mafia

> Contraband is our cultural patrimony.
> —Ivan Kasttrev

Historical Links Between the Mafia and Capitalism

In the last few decades, the mafia—which previously inspired masterpieces of film and literature and a thinly-disguised aura of admiration (from robbers to pirates to the Italian-American mafia)—has left the page and the movie set to become one of the world's primary security threats (Ruesga & Resa, 1997). What has led to this change? In an attempt to address this question, we've decided to explore the historical relationship between organized crime and capitalism. In the present day, these criminal networks can be considered the most visible and representative feature of gore capitalism.

Beyond the mafia's pivotal role in globalization and the contemporary exacerbation of consumerism, we can trace the relationship between liberal economies and organized crime back to the eighteenth century. By that time, pirates—especially British ones—"had been transformed into powerful businessmen who invested their illegal profits in the legal economy, thus allowing that legal economy to prosper" (Ruesga & Resa, 1997). This influx of resources gave rise to industrialization and to capitalism itself. Other examples of this amalgamation of crime and capitalism are evident in the United States and in post-Civil War Spain, among others. In the first case, we find the "robber barons, whose participation in industrialization and even in the nation's own construction was essential in the United States" (Ruesga & Resa, 1997). In the latter case, Carlos Resa tells us:

In post-war Spain, the worsening economy, international isolation, the weakness of the State, and the lack of consumer goods in the Spanish economy contributed to the strengthening of a preexisting form of organized crime, in which the trafficking of military cigars during the African War played an essential part. As an homage to its inventors, it was called *estraperlo* [straperlo]. The concept included a wide range of illegal activities including the black market for primary goods, payments for illicit services, extortion, threats, and mafia taxes in a context of widespread corruption. This was the product of the incredible arrogance of the victors of the Civil War, the principal actors in this drama, along with merchants and industrialists. Straperlo disappeared as soon as rationing came to an end and the main businessmen involved in illegal trading became respectable owners of companies in construction, finance, and other arenas. (Ruesga & Resa, 1997)

It is inarguably true that violence is the order of the day and that organized crime has infiltrated our lives in almost imperceptible ways beyond the news, televised entertainment, or the tabloids. We must keep in mind that this reality did not occur spontaneously, but rather it has developed over the last few centuries in conjunction with a series of related phenomena. What's more, it has become increasingly extreme over the last two centuries due to phenomena that might seem unconnected and innocuous, but which have laid the groundwork for its global development and dissemination. Some of these situations seem so random and distant from each other that it is difficult to understand how they have directly influenced the globalization of crime and the entrenchment of power as an extremely profitable way to acquire capital quickly and efficiently.

Now, quoting Misha Glenny, we will point out some of the primary situations that have led to the ascent of what we've called gore capitalism:

The post-World War II order began to crumble in the first half of the 1980s. ... There was one development, however, that had its roots firmly in America and in its primary European ally, Britain. The world was taking its first steps toward the liberalization of international financial and commodity markets. Western corporations and banks had begun to pry open markets that hitherto maintained strict controls on foreign investment and currency exchange. Then came the fall of Communism in 1989 ... Out of ideas, short of money and beaten in the race for technological superiority, Communism fizzled out in days rather than years. This was a monumental event that fused with the processes of globalization to trigger an exponential rise in the shadow economy. These huge economic and political shifts affected every part of the planet.

Overall, there was an important worldwide upsurge in trade, investment, and the creation of wealth. The latter was, however, distributed very unevenly. Countless states found themselves cast into the purgatory that became known as "transition" ... In these badlands, economic survival often meant grabbing a gun and snatching what you could to survive. (Glenny, 2008, xv–xvi)

Economic violence thus became a decisive factor in shaping and popularizing gore capitalism as a means of survival. As years passed, the use of violence as a tool for subsistence opened up new ways of harnessing it, bringing together workplace precarity, existential precarity, and marginality with a new way of thinking of violence and crime as transnational businesses.

The New Mafia as Transnational Business

As the interpretative paradigm of crime began to shift at the hands of endriago subjects supported by the most savage form of neoliberalism, criminal organization took on an unimaginable force. They were entered in the majority of economic circuits: from the gray or black markets where the drug trade, illegal arms-selling, prostitution, and money laundering had historically been confined to legal economic markets like construction, entertainment, international investment banking, private security, and privatized military services.

Thus, "criminal activities, as in the paradigmatic case of the drug business, do not escape the rules that govern the *new economy*" (Curbet, 2007, 71). The old structures of the mafia have been altered, as large-scale criminals and mafiosos of all types come to see themselves as business owners. These are business owners who form "a clan made of violent company men and killer managers, of builders and landowners. Each with his own armed band and linked by economic interests" (Saviano, 2008, 208). Their motivation is no different from that attributed to "honest" businessmen: attain the highest possible profits for their businesses.

In the contemporary moment, organized crime and the mafia can be discussed in the same way we would discuss a well-organized business: as a multi-level corporation, "a rational economic phenomenon, which as an industry boasts of having a structure and a mode of operation that are very similar to its counterparts in the legal economy" (Curbet, 2007, 70). In the case of the drug trade, it is divided into four basic levels that are then subdivided according to each cartel's specific needs. As Resa explains:

> In fact, organized crime is the ideal model for a business organization. It is structured on a well-perfected system of networks, which are the most efficient and most promising of models. It creates bonds of loyalty throughout the business and its workers, who are quite often of the same ethnicity. (Ruesga & Resa, 1997)

At the organization's first and highest level, we find the bosses who serve as financial backers and managers, while they also control drug trafficking through their direct affiliate henchmen. At the second level are the individuals who directly handle the drugs, that is the people who buy, prepare, cut, and distribute them to the cartel's local representatives. At the third level are these individuals and the *jefes de plaza* [local bosses], who are in direct contact with the dealers; they devise escape plans, coordinate security, and safeguard the location of the merchandise and the labs where the drugs are processed. The fourth, lowest level is the one the public sees and is the most well-known and identifiable by society-at-large: street-level dealers.

This last level is influenced by rising levels of workplace precarity and subcontracting. At this level, the cartels take advantage of chronic unemployment and the lack of social development projects by neoliberal governments, both in the Third World and the First. Subcontracted by criminal organizations to work in the lowest level of the pyramid, these workers are usually young (and mainly male), individuals who have been seduced by the hyperconsumerist drive into signing up with these criminal groups. This fact is no accident, as Roberto Saviano explains:

> The advantages for the clan are many: a boy earns half the salary of a low-ranking adult, rarely has to support his parents, doesn't have the burdens of a family or fixed hours, doesn't need to be paid punctually, and above all, is willing to be on the

streets at all times... These baby pushers are fundamental to the flexible economy of drug peddling because they attract less attention... (Saviano, 2008, 105)

Beyond the aforementioned levels within the organization, we must also remember that all the cartels have their own military teams. Normally, these teams are made up of former army special forces, elite former athletes—especially wrestlers, football or hockey players, i.e. people with an intimidating physicality—former gang members, and the like. All these individuals form a terrifying force, tasked with protecting the different levels of the cartel, preserving it as a stable economic-financial structure.

In addition to the transformation of the cartel into a multilevel corporation, these organizations have set aside old mafia codes, updating the roles of its members. Given the neoliberal, corporate Darwinist logic of the cartels, their leaders must be younger and younger. Currently, according to data reported by the Mexican media, the majority of new Mexican capos are no older than 35. Driven by a turbulent euphoria, they attempt to equate being a winner with youth, since "the market doesn't make concessions for the appreciation [over time] of human assets" (Saviano, 2008, 75). Thus, this new type of mafia wrings out all the human capital it can without wasting a drop and, in addition, carries out a risk-benefit analysis that would be the envy of any brokerage firm. At a time when the market is less than perfect, when monopolizing tendencies—which are a natural part of any market—abound, and when there is an almost complete lack of clarity about what is permissible and what is not, business activity that aims for effectiveness can have no scruples, neither social nor of any other type. Without a doubt, organized crime is the most well-developed and refined form of business in an unregulated market, or put another way, it is a market controlled by an elite, in which money confers the only legitimate source of power, which is exercised arbitrarily by those who wield it. (Resa, "The Russian Mafia," 2003)

This new structure of the corporate mafia responds to the new reality in which "now they were all on the same level: no appealing to a mythical past, previous experience, or respect owed. Everyone had to get by on the strength of his proposals, management abilities, or charisma" (Saviano, 2008, 75). Breaking with the cryptoreligious atavisms that the old school mafia was based upon, the new mafia views the previous respect for the lives of their adversaries' women and children as an obstacle in the race for dominance. Intimidation and warnings are now seen as insufficient, as out-dated notions and ineffective injunctions. The only limitations recognized by the new mafia are those imposed by the law of supply and demand.

Using the dynamics of transnational markets for guidance, the criminal enterprises and their operators form global alliances, adopting the structure of transnational businesses with "branches" around the world. Thus:

> What is known by the name transnational organized crime [is] a concept that encompasses several more or less hierarchical criminal groupings that feature different levels of collaboration between one another. Specifically, the terms group together Latin American and Asian drug traffickers, the Italian Mafia in its process of accelerated expansion, the Japanese Yakuza, the Chinese Triads and that scattered mishmash that is the alliance between criminal and political elements in Russia and other Eastern countries. (Glenny, 2008, xvi)

The restructuring of mafia organizations is also visible in their efficient, profit-oriented control of media information. We see this at two levels: first, through unpaid advertising and second, through the leaking of information about the strategies developed by law enforcement in different countries in their anti-mafia departments. In addition, the media includes information about the techno-logical advances being used worldwide to administer increasing economic globalization.

The growth of lawful trade flows, advances in transportation and communications, and greater porosity of borders have allowed for the circulation of illegal goods and services.

> One of the most obvious effects of these techno-logical advances has been the acceleration of migratory processes and the gradual creation of ethnic networks. These networks have spread around the world using cosmopolitan cities as their hubs, since these places guarantee anonymity. [These] ethnic diasporas have catalyzed the development of transnational criminal networks with constant contact across said networks thanks to the modernization of communications systems. (Resa, "Transnational Organized Crime")

Born in the society of the spectacle, these criminals see the media as a crucial tool to promote them-selves and their status, and the media provides them with publicity and legitimacy—at no charge—through the spectacularization of vio-lence. In addition, the media instills a deep sense of fear in the population, and the criminals under-stand this fear to be another way to propagate their own power and control over the territory.

A clear example of this use of the media and publicity by organized crime is found in the case of the Mexican drug traffickers who make up the cartel called *La Familia*, which is based in the state of Michoacán in the southwestern part of Mexico:

> The capos of La Familia are also pioneers in another respect: publicity. It's not enough to just kill someone. It has to be done in the bloodiest way possible and with publicity. According to a police report that cannot be reproduced because of the sheer brutality of its images, La Familia has a real media strategy. After killing their rivals, they cut their heads off and display them in public places alongside messages threatening their rivals—mainly Los Zetas—and even informing them who will be next to be killed. In a video distributed over the Internet, one can see the execution of an alleged member of Los Zetas. He appears practically naked, tied to a chair, wearing only a pair of black underwear and with menacing phrases written all over his body. Nonetheless, La Familia's messages are not only directed at the rival cartels, but also at the general population; as incredible as it might sound, they also take out paid advertisements in the main newspapers. Their objective: to win the sympathy of the citizenry. How? Once again, by taking on the functions that used to belong to the State.

One of the messages inserted onto a full page of *La Voz de Michoacán* and in *El Sol de Morelia* says: "Our mission is to do away with kidnapping, in-person and telephone extortions, contract killings, robbery … Perhaps right now people don't understand us … Unfortunately, we have used very severe tactics, since they are the only way to bring order to the State and we won't allow things to get out of control." (Ordaz, 2009)

The media's work to instill fear among the citizenry does not require any direct investment, energy, or capital from the criminals, yet it yields significant benefits not just for them, but also for the media, governments, and the market, stimulating a process of capital creation for this economic criminal empire.

In its quest for an ever-larger audience, the media becomes an accomplice of organized crime, necessary cogs in the machine to spread and popularize gore capitalism. This produces increased economic benefits as well: "the press abandons any sense of ethics as they pursue that segment of the market that devours crime news with a wild ferocity. The pleasure they take in violence and in the spectacularization of civic fear would appear to hide both a moralizing undertone and a spreadsheet with evidence of their economic salvation" (Saavedra, 2008).

We can conclude that the new mafia complicates the previous structures of criminality as they efficiently adapt to transnational economic demands and to the promise of a welfare state left behind by the nation-state. Thus, "organized crime represents a refined form of [gore] capitalism, a form that is regulated neither by law now morality and which therefore is an especially efficient means to accumulate capital" (Ruesga & Resa, 1997).

Overspecialization of Violence

The Concept of Creative Destruction

In the 1940s, Joseph Schumpeter introduced the concept "creative destruction" into economics.[1] This term referred to the process of innovation that takes place in a market economy whereby new products destroy old companies and business models. According to Schumpeter, the innovations created by entrepreneurs are the force that drives long-term, sustained economic growth. Nevertheless, he did not ignore the fact that this economic dynamic was based on the destruction of what has already been established, that which had to be overcome by new processes. According to him, it is in this process of creative destruction where the essence of capitalism is found. Likewise, the innovator-entrepreneur embodies the power to create markets. Schumpeter's entrepreneur comes from any social class and dreams of creating an economic empire, an entrepreneurial dynasty.

Schumpeter's concept is directly linked to the overspecialization of violence both in its military incarnations as well as the violence exercised by endriago subjects. If we analyze the processes of the markets created by gore capitalism, we see that they exactly follow Schumpeter's process of creative destruction. Bolstered by a theorization that absolves any guilt or responsibility for the most ferocious provisions of capitalism, overspecialized techniques to inflict violence have become objects of consumption.

It is undeniable that the overspecialization of violence has its roots in military tactics and their development for warfare, since as we know, "warfare [is approached] as a vast engineering project whose essential processes are as precisely calculable as the tensile strength requirements of a dam or a bridge" (Watts, 1984, 106). Thus it could be argued that gore capitalism's creative destruction can be read as a discipline based on the application of technologies of pain on bodies in blunt and sometimes fatal ways; in doing so, no moral judgments are permissible as these are seen to be solely economic issues.

Violence as Economic Discipline

It is no secret that violence is an inherent part of the human condition. Nevertheless, within what we are calling gore capitalism, forms of exercising violence have become hyper-specialized—founded in an instrumentalist and economist rationality— designed to inflict pain, to torture, and to kill. The more "sophisticated," pre-planned, and militaristic these methods become, the more repugnant and despicable they are (from any point of view). In gore capitalism, traditional weapons have been converted into ancillary tools compared to new methods, which assume an increased level of cruelty. These methods—founded in extreme ferocity and efficacy—become means to deploy, reinforce, and preserve their powers of intimidation; thus, they create a reticular and managed terror, transferred from the bodies of the injured and murdered into the bodies of those who have not yet suffered such violence.

Research into the most effective and cruel methods of torture and killing leads to the introduction and implementation of a series of techniques including decapitation,[2] dismembering, immersion into pools filled with piranhas or crocodiles, or into acid (which dissolves living victims into practically nothing). What has been fashioned is a semiotics of violence and a *signature* specific to each mafia organization.

In this respect, the mafia conceives of itself as meaningful within market logics and looks to establish itself as a *registered brand* (™), capable of spinning off its own branches and franchises. In Russia, Misha Glenny has noted that the Chechen mafia—known as the McMafia because of its transnationalizing power—has established itself as a franchise. With its reputation as the most violent and bloodthirsty mafia in the world, it was able to commercialize its name among external individuals who were looking for a way to legitimate themselves in the criminal business, creating a new market niche devoted to criminal fashions that are based on the supply and demand for *violence specialists*.

This phenomenon can seem especially absurd from the point of view of those of us who do not participate in the deployment of violence as an economic discipline. Nevertheless, these trademarks have already been adopted by a variety of criminals worldwide. For example, Mexican drug traffickers enact a particular style of violence that they link to *a signature* or *a brand* in underworld tradition. For example, it is widely known that the Tijuana cartel—also known as the CAF (Cartel Arellano-Félix) "works" by emulating the style of the Sicilian mafia. The Cartel del Golfo [Gulf Cartel] defends their own style, forging their *criminal signature* through a private army made up of Mexican and Salvadoran ex-military men, *Los*

Zetas, who murder their enemies in the style of the *Mara Salvatrucha* (extremely violent Salvadoran ex-guerrillas known for their penchant for decapitating their victims).

This style of criminality has been visible in Mexico since 2001. As the rules governing this realm have changed, pre-existing codes of honor—including exemptions for women and children—have gone by the wayside. Now the only moral code is dictated by the economy, which requires the capacity to kill with no distinction for gender or age, as long as this lack of moral boundaries increases profits or improves competitiveness. This is the totalizing effect of a mafia that bases its work strictly on the dictums of the most ferocious form of neoliberalism, wedded to transactions, the settling of scores, and profits above all else.

Within the logics of profitability and exclusivity that the market uses to drive consumption, international mafias have created their own *individual trademarks, offering a personalized product*. In the case of Mexican organized crime, this trademark is developed through the deployment of gruesome, sensationalist, and bloodthirsty practices of violence: gore violence, which seems to be inspired by Hollywood movies, but ends up being a specific brand for each cartel. This overspecialized violence is taken beyond the limits of the imaginable (outside of the contexts of war) as a way to make a name for oneself and to attain a certain respectability within the gore marketplace.

When we speak of the overspecialization of violence as an economic sector, we are not referring only to torture satisfying the torturer's sadistic impulse and enjoyment, but also a dystopian rationalization of the violence. The motives behind the killings or the torture are not obscure or personal, but rather are understood to have a clear economic motivation. This converts these practices into a type of "normal" work in the era of the *gore precariat*.

Piracy of Crime: Violence Specialists and Opportunists

We use the term *piracy* in its most expansive property sense, which we define as the copying and unauthorized distribution of works without the permission of their author. We think this definition is necessary to begin to deal with the phenomenon of the piracy of crime that emerged in the last few years at the margins of criminal organizations.

What has arisen is a *piracy of organized crime*, which became increasingly common beginning in 2006, especially in regard to kidnapping and extortion. Anti-crime officials distinguish between *professional* criminals and *pirate (or fake) criminals*, with the latter being the more dangerous and sadistic of the two. This is because pirate criminals are unaware of the methods followed by professional criminal organizations when carrying out kidnappings, leading pirate kidnappers to use violent and amateurish methods, usually resulting in the death of the victims.

The paradox is clear: dividing criminals into *professionals* and *pirates* tells us that crime itself has become an integral part of the deepest structures and daily lives of citizens. At least in Latin American contexts, this is an inescapable reality. On the one hand, this division speaks to us of the proliferation of opportunism in contexts with high levels of criminality and existential, social, and workplace precarity. On the other hand, the normalization and professionalization of crime carried out by government security forces is evidence of the extensive overlap between these legitimate institutions and organized crime. What becomes especially clear is the close relationships between government and violence specialists, since in many cases the government itself has trained them in their areas of specialization. Thus, it is not surprising that, as Charles Tilly argues:

> Where participation in organized violence opens paths to political and economic power, collective violence multiplies. Most notably, power seeking by violent specialists promotes the types of violent interaction I have called coordinated destruction and opportunism. Specialists in

violence do not simply deploy damage for the pleasure of it or for the profit it brings them; they use violence and threats of violence to pursue projects of their own. (Tilly, 2003, 41)

One problem with this division between violence specialists and opportunists is that it neglects to consider how we might explain the fact that the illicit appropriation of the body of the Other has become a kind of currency.

It seems illogical to criminalize the exercise of violence by *unauthorized criminals* more harshly than others. Nevertheless, the proliferation of criminals with unforeseen characteristics and within frameworks unrecognized by the authorities makes the issue of endriago subjectivity more complex. It also makes the State's battles against said proliferation essentially futile.

In their actions, the variety of players within gore capitalism illustrate the contradictions, reinterpretations, and anguish found in their own contexts. The endriago subject who participates actively within gore capitalism likely emerges out of a context of real need. Yet, we argue that the dyad of poverty and violence is more complicated, and this means that these violent actions are also a manifestation of a broader expression of social unrest, since "crime, besides generating additional profit, is also a means to express discontent" (Resa, 1997).

We know that economic inequality is an important factor—though not the only one—in the exercise of criminality. The process that leads to violence is made up of a composite of elements that include but are not limited to poverty; at the same time, we assert the importance of social inequality and poverty as pivotal to the exercise of criminal violence. Nevertheless, we agree with Resa that in order to create a criminal network, one has to possess the technical and economic means to bring it into operation. Thus the exercise and administration of violence—understood as a product—is based on a brutal hierarchy, within which the poor—those who do not have access to the means of production—contribute their labor power in order to occupy the lowest, but most important, rung of the criminal ladder: those who carry out the violence itself. Besides economic survival, these individuals are motivated by a desire for mobility and social belonging provided by the legitimacy that comes from money. Thus, what results is a type of *new proletariat of violence* or *gore proletariat.*

The overspecialization in violence as a distinctive element of endriago subjects means that they take the body and its abuse as a commodity in a literal and postmodern sense; namely, these subjects locate the body "within the cultural logic of late capitalism" (Jameson, 1995). This logic demands the constant, frenzied production of novel goods that are far removed from systems of powerful thinking like, for example, ethics.

In the 1970s, Deleuze and Guattari argued that our societies produce *schizos* the same way they produce Ford cars, the difference being that *schizos* cannot be sold.[3] Almost four decades later, capitalism—having transformed into gore capitalism—is not only producing *schizos* but also contract killers, specialists in violence itself. These specialists have found a way to reformulate space, the body, and death, transforming the ability to make another human being die into a capitalizable phenomenon, even outside of wartime. They have made violence into another market niche, recontextualizing the position of the *body as a strategy for accumulation*.

The Semiotics of Violence: Torture Techniques

The development and exercise of overspecialized violence is rooted in a more global history: in the history of State technologies for disciplining the body. In the contemporary gore era, these techniques—developed by the State and imparted to their military apparatus—are offered in the marketplace as goods and services. At the same time, these technologies of *vicious meticulousness* introduce a code for reading within the framework of violence, giving rise to a semiotics of violence itself through the interpretation of messages sent through the application of specific techniques of torture and modes of killing.

In this vein, we should mention the case of the Mexican drug cartels, which, according to statements by George Friedman (the director of the U.S. security consulting firm Stratfor), want to "project an image of overwhelming power and the killings, the threats, and their messages are a public demonstration of what they are capable of doing" (Alvarado, 2008).

Moving forward, we will mention some codes linked to the semiotics of overspecialized violence in gore capitalism as exercised by the Mexican drug cartels:

> To be executed at point blank range implies a desire to impart a lesson. If the body shows obvious signs of torture, it means that information had to be obtained from that person. Being wrapped in a blanket after the killing denotes an affinity with the dead, probably because the individual belonged to a rival cartel in which he was known or respected. Killing someone with a plastic bag over their head to asphyxiate them represents the desire to inflict pain slowly over a long period of time. A body that has been wrapped in bandages means the same thing as the previous code. A

body with its hands bound means the person was prepared for their execution. If the body has bandages on the feet or hands, it denotes torture to obtain information. Eyes bulging out of the sockets means the person betrayed the cartel, most likely a police informant. Amputated fingers mean information was leaked to another cartel. Bodies dissolved in acid denote economic debts to the cartel. (González, 2008)

As orchestrated by Mexican drug traffickers, these signals re-conceptualize the body as a cartography prone to rewriting, since the inscription of these codes of organized crime attempts to establish a macabre dialogue and a social imaginary based on constant threats. These inscriptions function as direct warnings, because "the message inscribed on [...] flesh [is] perfectly clear to everyone" (Saviano, 2008, 130). For the violence specialists of gore capitalism, *the lacerated and violated body is itself the message*.

These acts make clear that not only the civil covenant has been broken but also the taboo of "the horror of the corpse as a symbol of violence and as a threat of the contagiousness of violence" (Bataille, 1986, 45). Once this taboo has been breached, we quickly stumble onto a stage of unimaginably brutal violence, located at the bounds of what is even defendable.

These practices also announce the absolute shift in the meaning of work and in its reinterpretation; work is historically a rational entity, one that excludes and prohibits the reproduction of violence and the violence of death.

The reinterpretation of work and human life to prioritize economic benefit also displaces any awareness of death; though previously this was understood philosophically as "the awareness we have of it" (Bataille, 48), now it has been reduced to the awareness of the power we must bestow upon it in order to obtain a benefit.

There has been an epistemological rupture in the conception of death; it is about to lose its very referent, at the point where trepidation and horror might be entirely lost. We are about to forget "the transition from the living state to the corpse [and the inherent gravity therein], that is, to the tormenting object that the corpse of one man is for another" (Bataille, 44). Gore capitalism subverts the known order and presents economic justifications for death itself.

Drugs

In the hyperconsumerist and post-Fordist societies we currently inhabit, the effects of drugs are manifold, ambiguous and above all pervasive. Drugs have become a self-administrable form of control over the body, and once inside us are transformed into a kind of *edible panopticon* that is assimilated into the body as a type of *microprosthetic control*. As Paul B. Preciado has noted, these drugs situate the body itself within the capitalist structure:

> Contemporary society is inhabited by [...] subjectivities defined by the substance (or substances) that supply their metabolism ... The success of contemporary technoscientific industry consists in transforming our depression into Prozac, our masculinity into testosterone, our erection into Viagra, our fertility/sterility into the Pill, our AIDS into tritherapy. (Preciado, 2013, 34–5)

Thus, these substances have become a part of our bodies and wield a certain power, as, in one way or another, they play a role in the creation of our subjectivities. This process is invariably linked to scientific research, to capital production and the creation of markets through their sale and consumption.

That said, the State and science have made a clear separation between legal drugs—medicines and pharmaceuticals developed by big pharma and provided with a medical prescription—and illegal drugs—all those substances derived from natural or synthetic sources (outside of Western medical and pharmaceutical protocols) that are self-administered, producing pleasure and dependence in the individual and distributed in such a way as to deny income and taxes to the state. This separation is driven by a residual aim to control, discipline and legislate bodies, but above all it has an economic objective.

The separation between legal and illegal substances is a measure taken by States as a result of their refusal to accept the hegemony of the drug market. This hegemony "wouldn't become explicit until the end of the twentieth century [and] has its roots in the origins of modern capitalism, transformations of medieval systems of production at the end of the fifteenth century that would open the way to industrial and colonial economies, to the biopolitical fiction of the nation-state and to regimes of scientific and technical knowledge" (Preciado, 2013, 145).

It's interesting that the consumption of drugs—which has been present since time immemorial in most civilizations (Escohotado, 1999)—was not the subject of legal regulations until the beginning of the twentieth century, when States began to address it as a taboo or, in the best of cases, as a public health problem.

In most cases, there has been a double standard in the approach to dealing with the drugs, since drug prohibition has meant increased profits for everyone involved in the trafficking of illegal drugs. These profits not only benefit illegal drug-trafficking organizations, but also the entire chain of corrupt officials, national governments and international governmental agencies that facilitate the process. It is crucial to remember, then, that "taxes on drugs have been the cornerstone of the modern State (since States can also become addicted to drug-related taxes) and the foundational financial pillar of European colonial empires" (Curbet, 2007, 67).

In the current moment, it could be said that the majority of us participate in the criminal economy, whether it be as consumers, dealers, subcontracted employees of one of the tentacles of these organizations or silent witnesses to this process.

Currently, "illegal" drugs show up in our lives in explicit ways, but their incorporation into our daily lives takes place on different levels and in interrelated ways through multiple uses. First of all, drug trafficking has been able to infiltrate and take root in entirely disparate geographies. On the one hand, countries with depressed economies, little state regulation, and high rates of corruption have used drug trafficking as a source of essential income for their GDP. On the other, even countries like Canada—rarely thought of as a country that produces illegal drugs[4]—have elected to join the scramble for profits under gore capitalism, since a minimal investment in drug trafficking can promise exorbitant profits.

Second, the rise of the existential and work-related precariat throughout the world has allowed drug trafficking to establish itself within the social fabric as a solution to chronic unemployment and the absence of social development projects. The drug trade has created another type of living, illegal economy, since "drugs … produce massive economic activity. They are a kind of machine in perpetual movement, that provides continuous work to the entire world, from farmworkers to lawyers and including doctors, police officers and therapists" (Curbet, 2007, 68).

Third, this new type of *living economy* ends up being extremely attractive to many subjects in the middle and upper classes as a kind of guaranteed investment that will yield higher and faster profitability than that offered by banks or traditional investments. Investing in drugs has become a *magic* formula for the bourgeoisie to augment their assets. Nevertheless, the entry of the bourgeoisie into the drug business has not been only as investors, but also as dealers within their circles of friends, giving drug dealing a new and improved look, ridding it of the taint of criminality. As a consequence of the loosening of the taboo against consumption and drug-dealing by unexpected social actors (like the First World petite bourgeoisie), the categories used to understand drug trafficking shift and in some cases disappear, leading to a discursive ambiguity.

Fourth, the *democratization* of drug prices and the new economic policies of the cartels have meant that certain drugs like cocaine, considered a chic drug in decades past, has turned into a drug for the masses, accessible to people of all income levels—depending on its level of purity—and capable of meeting all price points.

This change in cocaine consumption speaks to how drug consumption has been transformed and adapted to social and economic demands. It also shows us how its use can be diversified into all social strata and can be understood as a *self-administerable prosthetic*, frequently used as a form of leisure, but also on the job to increase productivity and to mediate demands for competitivity mandated by bosses, whether multinational corporations or in precarious conditions of exploitation.[5]

The *democratization* of drug consumption—which has become increasingly socially acceptable in this globalized era—stands in stark contrast to the double standard with which governments confront drug trafficking. There has been a consistent lack of clarity about the costs incurred as a result of drug consumption: not just the market price paid for each dose, but the additional price of the bloodshed. None of us can be exempted from our responsibility for this direct or indirect participation in the industry around drugs: not ourselves as citizens, nor our governments, which use moral judgments to avoid consideration of options that might meaningfully regulate this problem.

Governments and Drugs

The majority of world governments (the United States especially) argue for a zero-tolerance policy with respect to the drug problem. These countries do not take into account that drug policies might be anything other than a moral issue. Despite this, according to the economist Diane Coyle:[6]

> [T]here [is] no chance of a zero-tolerance policy working when so many citizens of our countries use illegal drugs. A law that more than one in five people (almost one in three Americans over the age of twelve) breaks at some point in their lives, and none of their friends will ever report them for, is a failing law. (Coyle, 2004, 8)

In Coyle's description of the issue, we see that a conservative approach to the drug problem gives rise to "civil disobedience," reinforced by the rhetoric circulating in the hyperconsumerist society and capitalist double standards.

Now, if we analyze the drug issue using economic theory, we find that the drug trade is an active market in which government restrictions have predictable effects: the more harsh prohibition is, the more profitable business becomes. This is simple to understand if we apply market logics based on supply and demand. Prohibition creates a monopoly, and this consequently produces violence between groups disputing control over the market and also criminality in the citizenry who are purchasers.

> [T]he policy of absolute prohibition—enforced by most governments that import illegal drugs—has created a parallel economy controlled by organized crime. The revenues generated by the drug trade need laundering, and extend the reach of mobsters into other, legal activities. This is a global economy, too. In the opinion of many experts, ranging from U.N. officials to Manuel Castells, the respected Berkeley sociologist, the growing reach of the criminal multinationals threatens to undermine legal, democratic institutions. It also certainly prevents the developing countries from aspiring to greater prosperity through traditional economic and political progress. Why should they bother when there is an easy source of cash earnings for their farmers, and one that happens to provide generous kickbacks for corrupt officials and politicians who turn a blind eye to the trade? (Coyle, 2004, 12)

The benefit is not just one-way, but rather is spread out between countries that are producers, transit countries and consuming nations through the development of political strategies based on the rhetoric of the drug war. It is no accident that the fight against drugs waged by governments, especially the U.S. government, continues to be a national priority; this fight is justified using moral arguments that conceal the benefits to the legal economies of these countries through the legal sale of weapons. As an example, take the case of the Mexican cartels who stock up on military weapons through purchases in all of the southern states of the U.S. along the Mexican border; these purchases drive the arms-based economy of the principal sponsor of the "war on drugs." The rhetoric of this drug war is quite straightforward, and its circular arguments become justification for an endless array of abuse of authority and sovereignty.

The United States and its "War on Drugs"

The goal of putting an end to drug trafficking has been translated into a war against drugs, waged by the United States and centered on Latin America since the end of the 1980s. This war is based on the idea of safeguarding and expanding U.S. hegemony worldwide:

With the fall of communism, a new mythical demon has been found in drug trafficking (of illegal drugs, of course, since distributors of legal drugs pay for their permission) and its first cousin, transnational organized crime. This has been made possible by the enviable assistance of fear-mongering disseminated in the media, with their stories about the grave risk faced by nations' social, political and economic systems. The extraordinary threat of the "Communist International" has been replaced with the fear of "International Crime, Inc." (Resa, 2003, "Macroeconomía")

As is well-known, capitalism uses morality to hide the ferocity of its economic strategies. The U.S. government's primary concern in the war on drugs has nothing to do with preserving life. The preservation of life is not a concern at all, neither the lives of consumers, nor those involved in the mafia itself. These lives are not regarded as "worth valuing and preserving, [lives] that qualify for recognition" (Butler, 2006, 34). Instead, what is valued by the government is the capital that bypasses the State through the illegal market and the possibility of implementing interventionist strategies of control at a global level.

Underlying the discourse of zero tolerance for drugs proclaimed by the U.S. is a justification for an interventionist policy that perpetually endeavors to control the countries "punished" by drug trafficking. Through the deployment of these policies of control, the U.S. creates a *state of exception* in these countries, at the same time as it increases arms sales to mafia organizations and permits increasing money laundering. According to Resa, the U.S. is the country with the highest capacity for money laundering, which necessitates a combination of factors for operations to be successful: "banking secrecy, underground banking systems, corruption, police resources and training in the monitoring of complicated financial operations, the presence of first-class financial centers, access to offshore banking havens and a level of control over foreign currency exchange" (Resa, "El crimen organizado transnacional").

This war on drugs is also used as a means to criminalize racial minorities using racist policies both within and outside of the territory of the United States. Additionally, it becomes an effective strategy for diverting State funds without needing justification other than the simple argument that the money is needed in the fight against the drug trade.

The war on drugs waged by the U.S. to control the drug trade within its own territory can be understood as an institutional tool that reinforces racism by controlling and restricting social and economic opportunities available to African American and Latinx communities. This war is undergirded by a "system of financial incentives that is built into the war on drugs, and because of the protection from prosecution [...] that white communities enjoy, this war in the United States is waged against blacks and Hispanics" (Glenny, 2008, 236).

It is beyond question that minority and under-privileged communities are doubly harmed: the fight against drugs seriously violates their civil rights and there is additional violence wrought by the movement of drugs through these communities, whose citizens find themselves in the crossfire between the government, drug-traffickers, and the effects of drug consumption.

The interventionist policies of control developed and implemented against racial minorities put these groups into a permanent state of siege. This situation consigns them to become both victims of violence and its perpetrators as well, as they are forced to develop strategies for survival in unfavorable conditions and to earn a living while dealing with both covert and overt violence. When we say covert violence, we include the international trade in human organs.

Among other contemporary realities, the global gore market, the poor administration of States, and advertising's imperative to hyperconsumption seem to normalize the message that violence is a necessary condition of the globalized era. Nevertheless, all of these economically-based reasons are not enough to allow us either to resign ourselves to accepting and consuming violence or to simply accept that violence is just another commodity in the global marketplace.

The Problem of Numbers in the Drug Business

Drug trafficking is an indisputably enormous industry that racks up billions in income, operates in all the world's currencies, and possesses a vast workforce, yet economists do not account for it as an industry in its own right, precisely because it is illegal. Nonetheless, they do admit that its sheer size and management practices have made it possible for the industry to both follow and redefine the laws of supply and demand.

When it comes to numbers that reflect the profits from the drug trade, we find huge contradictions, though in most instances it is insinuated that the sums of money generated by the industry are exorbitant. Nevertheless, official numbers contradict each other, depending on the entity that releases them (Resa, 2003). For example, the data offered in 1994 by the Deputy Attorney General for Mexico, Moisés Moreno Hernández, provides evidence of thirty billion dollars as the amount of income in Mexico derived from the sale of drugs both inside and outside the country; that number increased in 2008 to some fifty billion dollars flowing from drug consumption in the United States.

Nonetheless, verifying these numbers is difficult, since they are passed around from one agency to another and are repeated by the media, who are "keen to bestow an appearance of rigor on their stories through the random inclusion of any kind of statistic, unwittingly contributing to the distortion of the debate in favor of the interests of what has come to be referred to as the *military-industrial-drug* complex" (Resa, 2003, "El dinero adicto a las drogas"). To that end, Resa has pointed out that:

> According to official and academic figures, the volume of capital handled around the world in the drug trade varies from $300 to $800 billion. A huge range, clearly. If we believed these high numbers, the drug trade would surpass worldwide sales in textile products and automobile exports across the planet. The most oft-repeated number within this huge range originated in the academic world and received the blessing of the United Nations, which decided to repeat it far and wide: $500 billion dollars on a global level. Despite its methodological weaknesses, this number has obstinately refused to wane over the years. First mentioned in 1991, this same figure has been repeated unchanged up until last year, and most likely it will continue to be thought reliable well into the current decade. (Resa, 2003, "El dinero adicto a las drogas")

In light of this, the use and dissemination of specific figures is hardly innocent. In fact, the majority of these numbers tend to be used in the months leading up to the annual certification carried out by the U.S. government in regard to the levels of cooperation in different countries with respect to policies around illegal drugs.

Thus, the hyperinflation of the figures attributed to the drug trade is based on a pre-planned strategy by governments to divert funding from their state coffers. Nevertheless, upon further analysis, these numbers end up being difficult to justify since self-serving exaggerations abound:

> In principle, and despite what common sense might suggest, the valuation does not derive from total sales, but rather production. The conclusion is that throughout the mathematical calculations to arrive at the magic number of $500 billion dollars, a series of estimates are made from an array of figures that tend to be inflated in accordance with the bureaucratic needs of each official agency. The number of acres under cultivation is inflated, the yield per acre is overestimated, the value of the raw materials needed to generate the final product is skewed and losses throughout the process are overlooked... The final result is a number that, at the very least, reflects a real inconsistency. (Resa, 2003, "El dinero adicto a las drogas")

This inconsistency becomes even more clear if we take into account that:

> The value of drug consumption in the United States has never surpassed $70 billion. Using the same standards of consumption and pricing, it can be assumed that spending on illicit drugs in the rest of the worldwide market represents another $50 billion. Taken together, the drug addicts and casual consumers of the world spend about $100 billion to fulfill their desires. Consequently, the difference between this figure for consumption and the $500 billion in income attributed to drug traffickers can only be explained from an economic perspective in two possible ways. Either the $400 billion that does not appear on official accounting records has been transferred into a market that is both fiscally unregistered but also untracked (in a sui generis case of an underground economy) or investments made by drug traffickers on Wall Street have produced fabulous earnings that have quadrupled their business profits. This last possibility is contradicted though by the fact that the fortunes of Colombian traffickers, those modern-day vampires, amounted solely to about $500 million, according to calculations from the draft legislation on confiscation of illicit assets. (Resa, 2003, "El dinero adicto a las drogas")

In the previous quote, Resa reveals that $400 billion dollars in revenues is simply unaccounted for; this shows how States have inflated the scale of the "problem" to obtain budget revenues. "What they have done is fabricate statistics to the liking of the bureaucratic interests who themselves are paid to uphold the current prohibitionist framework and to inflate the size of the conflict to procure additional public resources" (Resa, 2003, "El dinero adicto a las drogas").

Thus, the appeal to numbers to deal with the problem of drug trafficking has to do with their capacity to articulate the emotions undergirding the social ideology upholding policies of prohibition and zero tolerance with respect to drugs; what results is a cyclical phenomenon of prohibition, consumption, and wealth creation for States and traffickers, unconcerned with the real social consequences of this type of economy.

Many economists, like Lev Timofeev, have spoken about the opportunities and benefits that would result from laws legalizing drugs in countries where spending on consumption is high. This legalization would, they argue, lead to the collapse of prices imposed by the black market and would dismantle the drug traffickers' monopoly on the market. This measure would have a domino effect on the global illegal economy:

If drugs that are currently illegal were legalized, if they were formally taxed and sold freely in stores, a large part of [the] problems would be resolved. A new path for development in Third World countries would come into view, and the United States would be obligated to use some other new stupid excuse to interfere in countries' internal affairs. And with the stroke of a pen, the profits of a number of banks would be diminished, along with their ability to hide their money laundering. (Resa, 2003, "Macroeconomía de las drogas")

Nevertheless, in this book, we will not delve too deeply into an analysis of drug legalization policies; rather, what we attempted to illustrate in this section is how the drug market has been fully incorporated into contemporary society. In doing so, we can more clearly examine the structures of gore capitalism as a system and scrutinize the economic logics underpinning the violence found in both legal and illegal economic systems. What becomes visible is the double standard inherent in economic policies established by States and their connections with illegal markets in the creation of the hyperconsumerist military-industrial-drug complex. This environment ends up being fertile ground for the proliferation and popularization of endriago subjectivities.

Borders

Borders as National Sacrifice Zones

Mike Davis has written about *national sacrifice zones*, using this term to think about the ecological disaster to which certain regions of the U.S. have been relegated, since neither these spaces nor their inhabitants are considered to be productive elements of the capitalist system. We will adopt this term to refer to the boundaries or borders between poor countries and powerful countries, spaces where a dynamic is established in which *anything goes* on either side of said border. These spaces are treated as the backyard of both countries: gate-territories and backdoor cities, where the undesirable and the desirable mix, hybridizing these elements and making it difficult to apply a traditional axiology for their conceptualization. In these zones, we find a kind of eschatological rupture that means they are thought of as self-devouring and uncanny.

According to Davis, "the uncanny ... involve[s] some 'return of the repressed,' as when, 'after the collapse of their religion, the gods turn into demons' [that is, into the undesirable or indiscernible]" (Davis, 2003, 7). Concepts of the *uncanny* and *fear* surround borders and, as Diana Palaversich has written, these ideas are used "as a metaphor for a series of liminal subjectivities experienced by individuals negotiating a variety of racial, ethnic, linguistic and sexual systems, ... this is not an abstract space but rather a space imbued with history and memory" (Palaversich, 2005, 173).

Speaking about borders always ends up being contentious since, on the one hand, these imaginary lines represent—paradoxically in a globalized world—hyperreal lines due to the high level of surveillance centered on them. On the other hand, these same lines are transformed into territories of postmodern discursive idealization. Nevertheless, borders are not reducible to their territoriality or to the discourses that take shape around them. Rather, they are a set of transformations and integration between g-local markets, work, territoriality, legal regulations, surveillance, languages, and the gendered and rationalized workforce. All of these elements intersect within the demands of the hyperconsumerist society under gore capitalism.

Although a kind of tangential identity is created along borders, this identity is not always hybrid, nor is it always dystopian. Nevertheless, we argue that borders are the perfect setting for the birth and growth of gore capitalism, since borderlands are forced to reinterpret the demands dictated by contemporary economic logics according to circumstances specific to border reality (in all senses of the term). Borderlands are also subject to the two-fold and often contradictory imperatives emanating from the two territories to which they belong. To say that all borders look alike is an unsustainable argument. However, when these borders unite/divide a wealthy country with/from an impoverished country, we find certain shared characteristics, since they "create markets that elude the states themselves" (Mbembe, 2002, 56). This process is "the basis for the emergence of alternative spaces that structure the informal economy, contraband and migratory movements. Far from being merely regional, these interstate exchanges are connected with international markets and their dynamics" (Mbembe, 2002, 56).

We must not forget the colonialist structures that undergird borders. This colonialism inserts itself into borderlands through the structuring of economic spaces that are plainly spaces of control and recolonization, since "one of the main legacies of colonization has been to set in motion a process of development that is unequal, depending on the regions and countries involved" (Mbembe, 2002, 61). While we are not appealing to a simplistic understanding of colonization, we do attempt to move away from positions that blatantly glorify borders as essentially hybrid and postmodern spaces. This position restricts us to malicious, reductive, and/or celebratory interpretations that bring together disparate poles like legos that can be assembled or disassembled; but this analysis neglects the very real physical effects of the border that impacts bodies through their deeply-situated socioeconomic and geopolitical conditions.

Given the fact that colonialist structures have been reestablished at a societal level, this time through consumption, it is logical that border cities would exhibit a new "heterogeneous and cosmopolitan urbanity [...] characterized by combination and mixture in clothing, music, and advertising as well as in practices of consumption in general" (Mbembe, 2002, 61–2). In these spaces, borders become transactional spaces of negotiation, re-appropriation, and limit-testing.

Since borders are often fertile ground for reinterpretation, it is unsurprising that borderlands are where certain movements—both creative and destructive—first take shape. Thus, we argue that borders are spaces that lend themselves to the creation of an eschatological scenario embodied by armed movements with ideologies of death and sacrifice or by criminal organizations with ideologies of death and consumption. These entities remix disparate and even contradictory elements in pursuit of their goals, "push[ing] to its ultimate limits the new cultural relationship between pleasure and death" (Mbembe, 2002, 63).

Thus, under the combined pressures of hyperconsumption, precarity and state constriction, new forms of socialization and authority arise in borderlands. These new forms recombine and re-configure the very concept of the periphery, sheltering and shaping endriago subjectivities that in turn become soldiers in full-blown non-State armies. This is the situation of criminal networks and drug cartels along the northern border of Mexico; what is forged there is a post-colonialism *in extremis* that melds the logics of consumption and frustration, positing overt violence and illegal practices as engines of radical activities of self-affirmation.

Tijuana as Capital of Gore

Much has been written about Tijuana since the mid-1990s. In fact, Tijuana has been the subject to over-representation and glorification in the realm of cultural studies and other disciplines following the famous statement by the Argentinean anthropologist Néstor García Canclini, who had this to say about the city: "[Tijuana is] a modern, contradictory, cosmopolitan city with a strong definition of itself ... this city is, along with New York, one of the biggest laboratories of postmodernity" (García Canclini, 2005, 233–4).

Even prior to the popularization and exoticization of Tijuana as the epitome of postmodernity, the city was already the object—in the Mexican social imaginary—of a *leyenda negra* [black legend] due to its location on the border. It has been said in these studies that *illegality* is a characteristic of borders, that these territories were created to play this role within the State. Be that as it may, these arguments do not contribute anything on a discursive level, since "naturalizing" the conditions of a particular territory leads to mystification and leaves us in an acritical and resigned position, negating the possibility that our actions might re-shape that supposedly essential "nature" of the place.

Tijuana has been the object of a kind of post-Orientalism that glorifies the re-interpretative dystopias of the economy and subjectivity as "radically open and new horizons: the insurrections of the peripheries show us that the inhabitants of the countryside are the living matter, the flesh of the crowd out of which the globalized world is made" (Negri & Cocco, 2007, 1).

We argue that any analysis of Tijuana must exist in dialogue with—and at the same time challenge—the three most common clichés about the city: *Tijuana, laboratory of postmodernity*; *Tijuana, city of crossings*; and *Tijuana, city of vice*. These clichés should not be disregarded, since we have to recognize that these facets of the city persist and are actually quite an important part of it. However, they cannot fully account for the realities that shape such a contradictory border, since they do not consider one of the fundamental epicenters of the city: its economy of violence. That is, these clichés do not help us to analyze the reach and the power of violence in Tijuana as a tool of necroempowerment and as a fundamental part of the global criminal economy that far exceeds the limitations of the postmodern fetishization of the city.

One of the most widespread narratives about Tijuana considers the city to be a laboratory of postmodernity, glorifying the city's hybridity, anomalous nature, and its illegality. One example of this is found in the following quote:

> Tijuana, instead of a city, more often than not, is a transa. The term comes from Mexican slang and within the border; the transa is experiencing a boom. Transa stands for agreement, bribery, business, intention, reflection and project. Transa refers to the illegitimate and what happens on the verge; not only of illegality but also of any non-conventional initiative. It is derived from "transaction." A transaction within another transaction—this is how Tijuana functions, Tijuana muddles up everything—Tijuana transa. (Montezemolo, Peralta & Yépez, 2006, 4)

Of course, Tijuana muddles up everything, but we do not learn what is muddled up, how this muddling up is accomplished, nor where these energies are directed. The use of this term only shows us a kind of metonymy out of all proportions whereby the city is transformed into "a maniacal scrapbook filled with colorful entries which have no relation to each other, no determining, rational or economic scheme" (Harvey, 1989, 5). If there is in fact an underlying scheme, this metonym does not bring any clarity to the matter.

While it is true that Tijuana makes existing paradigms fail, the city also participates in them, given the paradoxical character imposed upon it by its territorial location. In this sense, Tijuana is interpreted as a *ciudad de paso* or *city of crossings*. Nevertheless, we think it would be more appropriate to understand Tijuana as a *trans-city* given that this prefix implies a sense of displacement that is not only physical, but also linguistic and economic, juxtaposed with California cities considered to be "postsuburban metropolises" (Davis, 2002, 96). Tijuana emerges as a post-apocalyptic landscape, an indisputable product of neoliberalism, and at the same time it becomes a key city in the New World Order and reveals that this *New Order* is a long way from fulfilling any non-economic promises.

In Tijuana, contrast is an important category of analysis, due to its clear differences from its northern neighbor, San Diego (located just 12 miles away). Although the climate and geography are practically the same, the appearance of each city makes it seem like they were located on diametrically opposed parts of the planet. While San Diego—

also known as *America's Finest City*—prides itself on its buildings, bays and beaches, its southern neighbor is full of shoddily-built constructions. In Tijuana, golf courses sit beside shanties and a motley array of other structures that range from homes built out of scrap materials to gigantic mansions built in a style we could classify as *narcoarchitecture*. This contrast is not only found in the landscape and architecture of Tijuana, but rather it can be seen all along the Mexican border:

> The U.S.-Mexico border is the only one in the world where a poor country—in which even official sources recognize that 40% of the population live below the poverty line—"rubs up" against the biggest economic and political power in the world, along an almost 2,000 mile long borderline. (Palaversich, 2005, 173)

Its strategic geographic location and its proximity to the most influential economic and political power in the globalized world means that Tijuana becomes the ideal zone for distributing illegal products and services into the U.S. market, one of the most prosperous in history. The interpretation of Tijuana as a *city of vice* must be logged and classified in relation to First World demands for leisure and consumption. In the case of Tijuana, an analysis of the U.S. market is essential, since its market is considered the primary worldwide consumer of gore capitalism's services to satisfy both practical and recreational needs.

The services offered by gore capitalism and violence as the primary economic driver in Tijuana are predicated on the fulfillment and re-appropriation of the logics of the U.S. market. Thus, the paragon of capitalism has decided to create, drive, and support the growth of a new modality: gore capitalism founded on the administration of violence and the criminal economy as fonts of wealth, establishing them in countries with depressed economies. That is, gore capitalism has been created remotely from a distance to satiate the demands of the U.S. market, which has been able to set up branches and laboratories of illegality in Third World countries. These supply illegal services and dismantle the available spectrum of economic possibilities, relegating these nations to a single type of economy based on violence, bloodshed, and trading in illegal products and services.

It is undeniable that the economy of the Tijuana border is based entirely on the purveyance of these services; nevertheless, this is a growing market, because:

Organized crime is such a rewarding industry in [countries with depressed economies considered far from power centers and inefficient] because ordinary West Europeans [and U.S. Americans] spend an ever-burgeoning amount of their spare time and money sleeping with prostitutes; smoking untaxed cigarettes; snorting coke through fifty-euro notes [or $100 bills] up their noses; employing illegal untaxed immigrant labor on subsistence wages [...] and purchasing the liver and kidneys of the desperately poor in the developing world. (Glenny, 2008, 41–2)

It is unsurprising then that both illegal products as well as strategies for their distribution are becoming increasingly radical. Classical economic thinking about production, consumption, and its resulting capital no longer function, and the production process itself is subverted, converting it into something barely recognizable or interpretable. This reality makes clear the urgent need to retrofit concepts of political economy and its relations of production in order to develop an analysis of the contemporary phase of capitalism that we classify in this book as gore capitalism. In Tijuana, the application of this logic—as a lifestyle focused on getting as rich as possible as quickly as possible—has been popularized because of its apparent simplicity: make the highest number of contacts possible within the circuits of organized crime, convince the largest number of campesinos possible to grow drugs on their lands, arm oneself to the teeth, hire a team of contract killers, purchase judicial protections, bribe the highest number of customs agents possible, and so on. Of course, the structures of the mafia are actually much more complex. And yet, within Tijuana, the standards of the *Old School Mafia* have been superseded by a kind of *piracy of crime*, which focuses on building networks with a smaller reach than the professional mafias at a local level; still, they are able to yield substantial profits for those who decide to *work* within them. A modified version of DIY (Do It Yourself), or in any case an *entrepreneurial* attitude.[7]

In addition to boosteristic promotion of the artistic boom in Tijuana at the turn of the twenty-first century, the events of September 11, 2001 also re/directed, exacerbated, and subsequently revealed the deep integration of structures of the gore economy in the city.

On that day, there was a radical acceleration of the upsurge in violence and the escalation of surveillance and impediments to border-crossing. This day had a radically different impact on the Mexican side of the border than it did in the United States, where "its citizens were introduced to the 'desert of the real'" (Žižek, 2005, 2). Along the Mexican border, fear was no looming threat; the lockdown at the border caused an urgent need for economic survival that quickly became a desire for personal enrichment. Thus, new "businesses" were sought out along the Tijuana border, for example the kidnapping of Tijuana residents. This new practice became incredibly profitable, while simultaneously being acclaimed, repudiated, and capitalized upon by local and national news media. All of this made Tijuana even more bloody and wont to devour itself.

Prior to 9/11, the use of armed violence was limited almost exclusively to battles between drug cartels, but post-9/11 this same violence became an economic engine that spurred on the highly profitable kidnapping business. This boom has had a devastating and marked effect in every respect, including a series of semiotic changes on the urban landscape of the city. For example, a sign reading "Se vende" ["For Sale"] hung outside of a home no longer just meant that the property was for sale. Rather it became resignified, no longer indicating a simple economic transaction but rather a transaction attempting to save someone's life. The sign signaled that one of the people living in the house had been kidnapped, and they had to sell the property to pay the ransom. In recent years, the number of properties with "For Sale" signs on them has multiplied exponentially.

It is both unsettling and terrifying to find out—as has been uncovered on several occasions—that kidnapping gangs are formed and sponsored by the judicial system (at a regional and national level) and protected by a variety of law enforcement agencies, military officers, ex-military, and politicians. Access to citizens' personal information ends up being quite easy for kidnapping organizations that collude with bank and governmental agency employees, who provide them with details about potential victims in order to guarantee their ability to pay a sizable ransom.

In *the big postmodern city* of Tijuana, the urban landscape has been altered by houses papered with "For Sale" signs and by people carrying guns, a landscape that sadly seems like a re-creation of a film set for a gangster movie. This urban landscape might be thought to be fictional by observers in the First World, but today it is the reality for many cities associated with the gore capitalist system, forged by this New World Order.

In territories like these, we find clear evidence that neoliberalism has no idea how to posit any kind of model for social integration, other than that built through consumption or a distorted conception of work. In this environment, unlawful practices are bolstered and promoted as keys to commercialization. In addition, we find a new gore subjectivity that could be explained thusly: *becoming a murderer* allows an individual to have access to and to legitimate oneself within a consumption-based existence. These individuals join a new *criminal class*, the product of neoliberalism as adopted in Third World spaces, founded on the sale of violence and "accompanied by an orgy of consumption and decadent behavior" (Glenny, 2008, 52). This spiral of violence has absorbed many Third World cities. Given the frustration, corruption, disregard, hunger, and poverty engulfing the majority of subjects in economically-depressed countries, the rationale of blood and guns as a means to fully participate in consumerism ends up—despite being repulsive—increasingly comprehensible and logical as radical demands of the system of hyperconsumption.

Just as in post-Soviet Russian, the system of justice in Mexico—that is, if it can still be referred to as such, in light of the fact that annually only two out of 100 crimes committed are resolved—is controlled by mafia groups and businesspeople. The Mexican State has not openly abdicated its duty to maintain social control, though, in daily lived experience, sovereignty and State control is buttressed by drug cartels and bands of kidnappers. "[A] distinction between legality and illegality, morality and immorality, barely exist[s]" (Glenny, 2008, 58). It's interesting that the definitions for organized crime remain quite inexact despite its ostentatious level of visibility; it is also interesting that illegal transactions, like money-laundering and extortion, are conceived of as everyday practices (in certain spaces) because of the frequency of their use.

Violence is converted into a resource for the gangster to manage, produce, and sell; it has become the tool *sine qua non* to carve out a space on the capitalist ladder. In Tijuana, what is most visible is a "triangular conspiracy between oligarchs, bureaucrats, and organized crime" (Glenny, 2008, 59); the fusion of these three groups has been widely publicized—although it had been an oft-repeated secret for years—since it has been concomitant with the outbreak of ever more frequent wars between drug traffickers along the northern border of Mexico, and now even in the rest of the country.

Tijuana is a capital city of gore because it has efficiently implemented the techniques of gore capitalism. These can be understood as a kind of mash-up of spontaneous violent practices with other practices that require greater sophistication, carried out both legally and illegally, exceeding the bounds of what is allowable. These practices of overt violence can range from an attack on a car orchestrated by armed commandos in the middle of a public space in order to settle scores between drug cartels to ultra-specialized techniques using toxic, chemical, and radioactive waste materials. This is the case of an increasingly frequent practice known as *pozole*, which consists of placing people (presumably while still alive) into barrels full of acid in order to dispose of them; the acid dissolves bone and entirely eliminates the bodies of the human beings placed in it. This practice reflects the radical extremes violence has reached and the freedom and impunity granted to it in the public realm.

The war between the cartels has no laws that govern it beyond economic ones, since it is focused on preserving the market for drugs, or, as it is referred to in the language of the drug trade: maintaining control over the *plazas* [zones or territories]. Thus, though organized crime is invested in the logic of the free market, it also inverts this logic from its location at the margins of legality. It also recuperates and reinforces that logic by centering violence and instigates a re-evaluation of capitalist logic by positing its own *reloaded* version of it, its gore version: a willingness to use "any method to muscle their way into [the] market, including violence" (Glenny, 2008, 54).

The midwives of this new bloody form of capitalism have been the most (un)expected characters: unemployed campesinos, corrupt police officers, politicians, thieves, contract killers, members of the army, etc.

The illegal market already has taken over a sizable portion of the global market. The ongoing debate about whether to favor the illegal economy or not is resolved if we keep in mind that the legal economy is more expensive, and capitalism has taught us that high prices are not good business for the consumer. Capitalism has insisted that we should always be on the side of businesses that report the highest profits. Therefore, in the majority of situations, it is not surprising that the first choice for the new capitalists is the illegal market; it is also unsurprising that this new economic mode has been transplanted into and blossomed in territories that are geographically close to world economic centers, allowing for a reworking of the traditional relationship between center and periphery. Tijuana has fallen into lockstep with these demands; that is why now we are dealing with the harsh and very *real* effects of these new procedures.

Tijuana, then, can be considered a city subjected to the New World Order, a city that has become an example of a "counter-geography" produced by gore capitalism. We understand counter-geography in the sense that Saskia Sassen has given to the term:

I call these circuits counter-geographies of globalization because they are: 1) directly or indirectly associated with some of the key programs and conditions that are at the heart of the global economy, but 2) are circuits not typically represented or seen as connected to globalization, and often actually operate outside and in violation of laws and treaties, yet are not exclusively embedded [though this type of activity cannot be completely separated from these circuits] in criminal operations as is the case with the illegal drug trade. (Sassen, 2000, 523)

Until 2005, when the violence and massacres of the drug war intensified and became inescapable, Tijuana could be understood using the paradigm of a "city [as] an imperfect and carnivalesque improvisation that yields to the fluxes of a dynamic … environment: things are allowed to remain in a halfway real condition" (Davis, 2003, 8). Nevertheless, in 2009, what was ever more apparent was the simultaneous clash and the overlap between the First and Third Worlds, represented by this city both discursively and materially.

Tijuana endures/enjoys the increasing paranoia and lack of security of any big city under threat from a collectively-recognized danger: overt violence and unknown danger; the question is always who will be the next person to face it, and perhaps more so who will be the ones to perpetrate it. In addition to the conception of "the capitalist big city [as] extremely dangerous" (Davis, 2003, 8), we also must keep in mind that the effect of the flows of people back and forth across the border are effectively incalculable, since individual relationships with the border space multiply along with the attendant dynamics and functions of those relationships.

The spectrality of the discourse about terror and the paranoia utilized by the United States to subjugate and more effectively monitor its citizens moves beyond its condition as specter and becomes real in Tijuana. This spectrality is realized and enacted there in residents' very bodies, bodies that ontologically exist, die, and shed their blood. Under these conditions, First World anxiety is a lesser symptom in comparison to the endemic fear that inhabits people's very bones: "Yet the landscape of terror is also, as in Bosch, voluptuous and nearly infinite in irony" (Davis, 2003, 9).

Thus, in Tijuana, we have embraced a number of elements from our Northern neighbor, the United States: the obscene delight with fostering, interpreting, and carrying out destruction and violence as a luxury, as something pleasurable. From the South in Mexico, we have inherited the celebration of tragic feeling, a taste for sacrifice, desire, and tradition that do not separate daily life from the sacred in a Christian or binaristic way.

Meanwhile, in the postmodern city:

Too many people lost their way in the labyrinth, it was simply too easy for us to lose each other as well as ourselves. And if there was something liberating about the possibility of playing many diverse roles there was also something stressful and deeply unsettling about it. Beneath all that, lay the grumbling threat of inexplicable violence, the inevitable companion of that omni-present tendency for social life to dissolve into total chaos. (Harvey, 1989, 6)

The previous quote can be applied to different cities that have been labeled as postmodern. Yet, in Tijuana and in other economically-weakened countries, far from the melancholy or nihilism experienced in the First World, what we find is a certain restless vitality, a constant feeling that somewhere someone is cooking up the next strategy for survival. In this sense, these cities are no longer post/modern, but rather post/mortem. What we find is a kind of ominous happiness. *A disturbing happiness in the face of blood.*

Tijuana manifests a symbiosis between violence conceived of as an object of consumption—deeply engrained in U.S. society—with the violence of colonial models of sacrifice and violent repression. The violence of sacrifice is continuous and embedded in Western European traditions (i.e. the witch hunts, the Inquisition, etc.) and cultural traditions. A continuous history of economic- and religious-based violence can be traced through the conquest of the Americas to the present day. These practices seem to have persisted in an altered, neocolonial state through the brutality of the killings, that retain a connection with colonial violence. These killings ritualize brutal scenes of a violence that recalls the aesthetics of gore films; these scenes of violence are instituted in a resignified form due to their economic value and their profitability. In addition, these killings display the fact that they belong within the cultural structure and moral system in which they participate. The extreme violence shaking Mexico right now is hardly a horrible exception; rather, it is the consequence of mismanagement by corrupt and authoritarian governments, undeniable poverty, and the cultural models for both us as individuals and as a nation. These personalities have been shaped by "film and music rife with tragedy and resentment directed at a life that is both treacherous and inhospitable" (Bares, 2008); in addition, they have been influenced by the media, especially television news "with the gross delight it takes in fatalities and blood from the earliest hours of the morning until late in the evening, incidentally providing some spice during mealtimes (Bares, 2008). There are also connections to the construction of national identity with machismo as its backbone; this central position accorded to machismo is made manifest in "indifference in the face of danger, contempt for feminine virtues and the affirmation of authority at every level" (Monsiváis, 1981, 9).

Tijuana is the crystallization of an *episteme of violence* that makes the latter into a fantasy shared by the entire country:

Unfortunately, the game played by authoritarian governments with this bloody spectacle we have suffered through has ended up getting out of their hands, and this has turned us into a violent society all-to-familiar with crime. A society that even when not involved directly in crime still accepts it at some level. What's more it quietly anticipates that one day it might be able to capitalize on it somehow. (Bares, 2008)

Over the course of this section, we've looked into the various arguments that theorize Tijuana as a laboratory of postmodernity, a city of crossings and a city of vice; all of these frameworks end up limited considering that Tijuana is in fact the capital of gore. This is because its identity as a "hybrid" city is no longer based on the production of signs—though perhaps the city never really was "hybrid" because its most illustrious practices are impossible to narrativize in a text. Now, what we find in Tijuana is the ruthless outbreak of brute force on bodies and the usurpation of those bodies; this is a key moment in capitalism's process of becoming-gore. These bodies have been transformed into an absolute commodity, utilizing the most gruesome kinds of violence to explicitly categorize those bodies and life itself, whose exchange value is monetary and transnational.

4

Necropolitics

> It was a time for us when any daily occurrence was
> preceded by death.
> —Angélica Liddell. *Y como no se pudrió: Blancanieves*
> *[And Since She Didn't Rot: Snow White]*

We'll begin with a brief outline of the *state of exception* and the Italian theorist Giorgio Agamben's argument in this regard. Agamben examines governments' increased power during periods of *supposed* crisis. Agamben refers to these periods as *states of exception*, in which civil and individual rights can be diminished, replaced, and negated as the government demands more powers. Quoting Agamben, "In every case, the state of exception marks a threshold at which logic and praxis blur with each other and a pure violence without *logos* claims to realize an enunciation without any real reference" (Agamben, 2008, 40). Thus, Agamben's *state of exception* exposes how the suspension of laws during a crisis can become prolonged, turning into a generalized state, in which the object of biopolitics is *bare life (zoe)*, a term that denotes the "simple fact of living" common to all living beings—as opposed to the *bios* that refers to the categorization of political subjects.

For Agamben, Nazi concentration camps are an example of the loss of rights as a result of imposing an absolute existential precarity, reducing human beings to extreme vulnerability. In the global era, however, there are many more examples of this extreme infringement on personhood, visible everywhere from the public arena to the workplace and even in the most intimate spheres. It takes the form of the utter destruction of bodies stemming through predatory use and their incorporation into the deregulated neoliberal market as another commodity, from the sale of organs to exploitation as a quasi-enslaved labor force. In both cases, we lose our *property rights to our own bodies*.

To further this point, we need to delve deeper into a discussion of the body,[1] since the body is the primary target of necropolitics, and what the body entails is a complicated and problematic enunciation. Agnes Heller writes that "it was modernity itself that legally emancipated the body for the first time in recorded history, by extending the *habeas corpus* act (once a nobleman's privilege) to everyone in principle" (Heller and Feher, 1994, 16). In modern societies, the body represents at the very least a doubling nexus, that is "in the modern world—where the body was legally recognized by the *habeas corpus* act, and where simultaneously the major trends of social life aimed at oppressing, eliminating, silencing, sublimating, and replacing that legally existing entity—a social space lent itself to biopolitics" (Heller and Feher, 1994, 17).

From this analysis, we see both that the body is enunciated as a metaphor sublimated by politics, and that where biopolitical processes and the reversal of biopower occur, the awareness of and responsibility to *habeas corpus* becomes more meaningful. It is in the nexus of the body where subjects become subjected and, at the same time, it is the concept of possessing one's own living body that has activated the subjected subjects, since it introduces them into a field of action as active agents despite (or perhaps due to) the fact that power is *always operating on bodies*. Nevertheless, there is a third reading of power and the function of the body in hyperconsumerist societies: the body as an increasingly valuable asset as it is reinterpreted as merchandise, another modality of biopolitical governability, an aspect that has not been considered and that is based on the highest economic profitability and its function within necropolitics.

For necropolitics and endriago subjects, the body is fundamental because it is conceived of as a critical commodity, since this is what gore capitalism advertises. The body has a specific value, ranging from medical and aesthetic technologies to "take care" and "rejuvenate" it to the release of the body after it is kidnapped and a ransom is paid. The body's care, its preservation, its freedom, and its integrity are all offered to us as products. There is a hyper-corporalization and a hyper-valorization applied to the body, which has been transformed into a profit-making commodity. The market has capitalized life itself through this endangered corporality, as the body has become an ever-more-profitable commodity.

Paradoxically, at the same time the body's importance is sold as commodity to all of the subjected subjects of civilian populations, there is an inverse movement orchestrated by endriago subjects with respect to the body. These figures tend to desacralize the body, both the body of the other (in order to commercialize it as an exchange commodity or its death as an object of work) and their own bodies. They gamble with their bodies and purport to surrender them, following a suicidal logic that indubitably leads them to their own bodily destruction and the loss of their own lives. This is the price that must inevitably be paid within the logic of gore enrichment, grounded in the assumptions and logic of bank loans:

This is the new rhythm of criminal entrepreneurs, the new thrust of the economy: to dominate at any cost. Power before all else. Economic victory is more precious than life itself. Than anyone's life, including your own. (Saviano, 2008, 114)

There exists, then, a negotiation with death, whether this happens through the strict adoption of capitalist logics or in a syncretic way combining capitalism and ritual. This is the case with Mexican criminals who have recently endorsed a particular cult that worships death, glorifying and elevating death itself to the position of sainthood. This syncretism is inherent to gore capitalism, in the sense that a population constantly subjected to the pressures of death's proximity will look to renegotiate death's role in the context of their society or social group. This renegotiation achieves the additional goal of inserting endriago subjects into discourse. So it is no accident that this discursive articulation takes the form of a religious cult—the context of many endriagos (in the case of Mexico) is deeply religious—which allows for their own discourse to develop with faith as a primary element. Faith is at the core of religious discourse and this is, in principle, the only discursive form available to them. Examining prayers to Santa Muerte, what is noteworthy is that they do not ask not to be killed, but rather for their deaths to be quick. These endriago subjects have renegotiated the role of death in their daily lives, allowing them to become active subjects in their own relationship with death.

In the contemporary era, death emerges as the nucleus of biopolitics, which transforms it into necropolitics. Achille Mbembe argues in this respect that "the ultimate expression of sovereignty resides, to a large degree, in the power and capacity to dictate who may live and who must die. Hence, to kill or to allow to live constitute the limits of sovereignty, its fundamental attributes" (Mbembe, 2003, 11–12). As in the case of Agamben, Mbembe sees Nazi Germany as the perfect example of this sovereignty over death, though Mbembe identifies slavery as one of the first fields for the implementation of biopolitics. Furthermore, he points out that colonies have been spaces where necropolitical, colonizing governments have achieved the largest and most long-lasting establishment of a *state of exception*.

We agree with Mbembe in regard to his geopolitically- and racially-situated analyses of biopolitics; however, we will posit necropolitics in opposition to biopolitics, since it is inscribed in the same register as biopolitics, but radicalizes it. Necropolitics desacralizes biopolitics and commodifies the processes of dying. If biopolitics is understood as the art of managing people's lives, capitalist demands have made it so that living and all of the processes associated with it are converted into commodities, which includes what we understand as necropower, since this represents the management of the final and most radical processes of living: death itself.

Thus, our reading of necropolitics is situated in the contemporary moment, in a geopolitically-specific location and in a concrete case: that of endriago subjects, epitomized by the Mexican criminals and cartels that participate in the framework of gore capitalism.

Necropolitics is a reinterpretation and stark iteration of biopower and the capacity for upending it, based significantly on the logic of a *warlike clash of forces*. Necropolitics exercises a kind of freedom, "but it is a freedom that is constituted as the 'power to deprive others.' In effect, in war there are the strong and the weak, the clever and the naive, the victorious and the vanquished, and they are all acting 'subjects,' they are 'free' even if this freedom only consists of the appropriation, conquest, and submission of other forces" (Lazzarato, 2000). Necropolitics is important because it re-situates the body at the center of the action without any interference. The bodies of dystopian dissidents and ungovernables are now those which hold power over the individual body and over the body of the population in general— though outside of humanist and rational logics, but inside rational-commercial ones. They have created a power parallel to the State without subscribing fully to it, while they simultaneously dispute its power to oppress.

Nevertheless, the practices utilized by endriago subjects enact a distinct and dissident application of the concept of biopolitics; they carry it into the territory of necropower that, as we can see, does not entirely translate into the context and exercise of necropolitics as Mbembe envisions it. It goes further, embarking on a dystopian reinterpretation of their condition as free subjects and, simultaneously, subject to economic dynamics. Endriagos embody ungovernability, though—due to their internalization of global capitalism's demands for hyperconsumption—they cling to power, while simultaneously internalizing a heteropatriarchal discourse as a way to legitimate their identity and their social belonging:

Because the modern State works, it seems, like a kind of de-subjectification machine: it's a machine that both scrambles all the classical identities and at the same time a machine that recodes these very same dissolved identities, especially in a legal sense: there is always a re-subjectification, a re-identification of these destroyed subjects, emptied of all identity. (Agamben, 2004, 116)

Identity itself is reconfigured and re-subjectivized through the media, publicity, technologies of gender, and hyperconsumption.

In order to analyze necropolitics and biopolitics in the Mexican context, we must begin with the fact that, in Mexico, there is no unitary State "but rather at least two: the insurgent state and the legal one, and both have traits, characteristics and logics, both formal and informal, classical and non-classical" (Maldonado, 2003, 235).[2] Nevertheless, the characteristics of these parallel States have not been sufficiently studied within the field of biopolitics, in the sense that extreme violence and hyperconsumerism have not been considered structuring elements in the formation of dissident subjectivities that resist the State. Thus, this *parallel State* represented by national and international criminals reshapes biopolitics itself and uses necropolitical practices to seize, preserve, and capitalize on the power to *inflict death*.

The necropolitics of endriago subjects is a corollary of biopolitics with its goals of governing territory, security, and population, but extends it in a monopolistic way by exploiting three elements: 1) exploiting the territory's natural resources, 2) selling private security to guarantee the well-being of the population, and 3) appropriating bodies from the civilian population as exchange commodities or as consumers of necromarket commodities. The necropolitics of endriago subjects is advanced in ways that previously were unheard of, not because these practices are new but rather because in previous periods they remained below the surface. This new necropolitical exercise has managed to secure the power of the Mexican State by gaining control of its economy, as a result of the legal economy's dependence on the criminal economy.

Above all, the ascendance and radicalization of necropolitics is grounded in the reality that necropolitics appropriates techniques previously reserved for "legitimate" state actors. As we understand it in this book, necropolitics is unique in that it is enacted by endriago subjects breaking from their condition as subjects restrained by the State; thus necropolitics has a manifold character, since it is implemented both by illegitimate and legitimate biopolitical actors (the government, the State, hegemonic discourse) and it is legitimated through these. Nevertheless, the exercise of necropolitics by endriago subjects means that—despite the fact that it might have referents in State practices—these subversive and dystopian subjects transform and reshape it in its application. For this reason, it becomes a difficult phenomenon to address, one that demands a series of successive approaches since "after a while it no longer makes sense to refer to an initial context. The phenomena of violence produce a new context" (Pécaut, 2001, 10). "The history of these phenomena does not coincide with their origins, and often that history has a logic that, while not indifferent to their origins, operates differently, in their own way" (Maldonado, 2003, 232).

We want to make it very clear that the endriago is not a hero; neither is he a resistant subject, nor does he attempt to be resistant. Rather, endriagos are businessmen who apply and synthesize the most aberrant neoliberal demands and logics.

> The logic of criminal business, of the bosses, coincides with the most aggressive neoliberalism… You pay with prison or your skin for the power to decide people's lives or deaths, promote a product, monopolize a slice of the economy, and invest in cutting-edge markets. (Saviano, 2008, 128)

We oppose deifying individuals who use dystopian strategies in opposition to biopolitics. We do not see these people as resistant subjects, since they use the logic of consumption and markets to legitimate themselves through violence and killing.

According to Agamben, drug users (among others) are encompassed by a type of movement that subverts or resists governmental biopower and their biopolitical management (see Grelet y Potte

Moneville, 1999–2000). In some ways, this relates to the entire chain of drug production and consumption; however, Agamben does not explicitly consider the different links in this chain—from producers to distributors and bosses—and how each level works to subvert biopower. These individuals also engage in a type of dystopian subversion of biopolitics, located as they are within the sphere of necropower, the site of their own resistance to biopower and where they dispute its hierarchy.

From our perspective, however, it is not clear how the reification of self-destructive behaviors—like drug consumption, for example—might lead to the creation of potent subjectivities and, additionally, to a real resistance movement. It's undeniable that by consuming drugs they are subverting state power, by infringing the social regulations of anti-drug policies. Their consumption can be understood as an act of civil disobedience, but not as an act of resistance, because it buttresses necropower through gore consumption. To understand drug consumption as an act of resistance is to acritically adhere to the logic of the gore marketplace. Drug consumers *per se* cannot be understood as subversive subjects since they reinforce a hierarchy of subjection (embodied by another biopolitical specter: criminals), perpetuating the chain of subjected subjects albeit by another of the system's specters.

In our view, it is both dangerous and acritical to celebrate all types of subjectivity that differ from the norm as resistant subjectivities. When we do this, we negate any chance we might have of formulating subjectivities that oppose biopower with a genuine resistance in a non-dystopian way. This is evidenced by drug consumers (as in Agamben's example) or by the *new subjectivities* formed in the favelas of Brazil (see Negri & Cocco, 2006). If we celebrate all subjectivities without accounting for the multiplicity of their variants, contexts, and their consequent oppressions and anti-resistance elements—as in the case of gender, as oppression against women and sexism are often seen as unimportant struggles by these subjectivities—we run the risk of creating a catachresis that depletes actual resistance movements of their contents and real force. We must forego the temptation to romanticize and exoticize the other. We know it is difficult; however, the on-going construction of an auto-critical discourse is the means of approach to attempt to "establish/recognize the conditions for the appearance of subjects able to act critically in the transnational world" (Lins, 2003, 27).

What we would like to do next is to present our ideas about necropower, necropractices, necro-empowerment and thanatophilia within gore capitalism. We understand necropower to be the appropriation and application of government technologies of biopolitics to subjugate bodies and populations; its fundamental element is the hyper-specialization of violence, and its goal is to commodify the process of inflicting death on someone.

Necropractices, for their part, can be understood as radical actions that aim to create bodily harm. One necropractice is how these endriago violence specialists reappropriate State methods for eliminating enemies of the State in order to eliminate their own enemies. Other necropractices can be found in new and innovative technologies for killing. Over the course of recent decades, these necropractices have become more permissible, as they have given rise to new cultural understandings, allowing the use of exceedingly brutal and horrifying forms of cruelty that can be converted into spectacle through their consumption as televised entertainment.

Empowerment can be understood as the processes that transform contexts and/or situations of vulnerability and/or subalterity into possibilities for action and personal power, thus upending hierarchies of oppression. Empowerment is also used in the context of aid for social and economic development to refer to people who are the objects of development activities to strengthen their own capacity to control their lives. It can also be thought of as a political process in which human rights and social justice are guaranteed for a socially marginalized group. In this book, we will designate necroempowerment as processes that are modeled on empowerment processes, but reformulate them through dystopian practices (like murder and torture) to acquire individualized power and, as a result, illicitly enrich and perversely self-affirm themselves.

When we use the term thanatophilia, we refer to the predilection for the spectacularization of death in contemporary hyperconsumerist societies, as well the taste for violence and destruction, its desire to kill, and its attraction to suicide and sadism. We prefer thanatophilia over necrophilia, since the latter is understood to be a sexual orientation that focuses attraction on corpses. Nonetheless, it is worth mentioning that Erich Fromm in his 1973 book, *Anatomy of Human Destructiveness,* refers to necrophilia in a non-sexual way as the consequence of living a life without ever really being alive. For Fromm, necrophilia is the opposite of biophilia and it is, along with symbiotic fixation and narcissism, one of humanity's three greatest problems. According to Fromm, the lack of love in Western society leads to necrophilia. The necrophilic person lives mechanically, converting feelings, processes and thoughts into things. The necrophiliac wants to control life, to make it predictable. Fromm argues that, because the necrophile feels that the only certain thing in life is death, the person begins to long for death and to worship it. For Fromm, necrophilia is visible in the contemporary Western world in the facades made of concrete and steel, in modern weaponry and the nuclear race, in the idolatry of large machinery and technology (technophilia), the loss of resources through consumption and treating people like things (bureaucracy). Our use of the term thanatophilia is linked to Fromm's necrophilia, but differs in its application and context.

In conclusion, we ask ourselves the same question as Mbembe: is the concept of biopower sufficient in the present moment to explicate contemporary realities founded on necropower? The answer is that biopolitics has to be rethought contextually. In our case, we can say that there is a parallel between biopolitics as administered by the State and necropolitics as upheld by endriago subjects: in both instances, the preservation of power through the exercise of violence is fundamental. Nonetheless, the necropolitics of endriago subjects cannot be explained solely by comparing it with the State since the endriago subjects embody a tripartite condition. First, they appropriate the tools of power (managed by the State) through violence to necroempower themselves and thus fulfill neoliberal demands for hyperconsumption. Second, through necroempowerment, they question the efficacy of disciplinary society as it has been previously understood. Finally, these subjects have arisen—each in their own specific geopolitical context—out of the population to which the majority of subjected subjects belong, which also encompasses those who forge non-dystopian strategies for resistance. Thus, we think that in order to comprehend the logics of endriago subjects' necropower, we need to triangulate 1) the dynamics of biopolitical power exercised economically and in the heteropatriarchy, 2) the active, though subjugated, subjectivity of the civilian population, and 3) the crucial role played by advertising and the media in societies of hyperconsumption, since "this [new] capitalism functions in reality thanks to the biomediatic management of subjectivity" (Preciado, 2008, 51).

Biomarket and Decorative Violence

Biomarket

When post-Fordist theorists like Negri and Hardt speak of *biopolitical production*, they use this concept—with its tinges of Foucauldian thought—to explain the complexity of contemporary forms of capitalist production. Here we take up the concept of *biopower* and we extrapolate from it to discuss *necropower* as a way to draw attention to the contemporary transition from one form of production and consumption to another.[3] This transition from *biopower* to *necropower* effectuates "a transformation of the structure of life" (Preciado, 2008, 212).

This transition becomes especially visible in forms of consumption, where the shift subverts categories of traditional political economics and delineates a new cartography of *biopowers*, based on *bioconsumption* and surplus value. These strategies of subversion are a threat to life and ways of living, benefitting the market under a necropolitical regime. We use the term *biomarket* to refer to this displacement that radically changes both social and individual forms of action by limiting action to consumption. We use the term *necropower* to refer to the radical and perverse way that this shift has been implemented.

The best way to explain this shift is by using Foucault's arguments about *biopower* and its impact on the establishment of a new ontology—specific to gore capitalism—that originates in the (consumerist) body and its capacity for consumption. That is, we see the *biomarket* create an epistemological displacement that is incorporated into bodies themselves; it no longer originates in an external, authoritarian structure, but rather it has been incorporated into our corporal systems through our obedience to consumption.

In this sense, we agree with Paul B. Preciado when he distances himself from the Panopticon as a method of interpreting the transformation of power in the contemporary world, writing:

> ... we are faced with a mechanism that—without any change in its effectiveness—has reduced its scale to that of a biomolecular technology that may be consumed individually... It is a form of control that is both democratic and private, edible, drinkable, inhalable, and easy to administer, whose spread throughout the social body has never been so rapid or so undetectable... [T]he same relationship between the body and power: a desire for infiltration, absorption, total occupation. We could give in to the temptation of representing this relationship according to a dialectical model of domination/oppression, as if it were a unidirectional movement in which miniaturized, liquid power from the outside infiltrates the obedient body of individuals. But no. It is not power infiltrating from the outside, it is the body desiring power [to consume], seeking to swallow it, eat it, administer it, wolf it down, more, always more... (Preciado, 2013, 207)

This transformation in power relations—between power and the body of the subject—participates in the emergence of what we might call here *consumerist power*, which will allow us to explicate the contemporary levels of unbridled consumerism, which has become hyperconsumerism.

In this section, we attempt to understand the *biomarket* as an epistemological category that might enable us to decipher neoliberal capitalism and its demands and practices of consumption. Of course, these cannot be deciphered if divorced from a system of market *bioassimilation* that (artifically) (re)produces, introduces, and compiles our consumption preferences.

We should remember that the *biomarket*—as a system—can no longer be understood as an external or hierarchical apparatus, but rather as a fluid structure that shifts in relation to our tastes and demands, creating a double helix similar to a strand of *consumption DNA*. It is impossible to analyze this double helix in a linear or genealogical way.

Our apparently voluntary consumerist behaviors contribute to the creation of products that enlarge market niches. For example, there are products considered *alternative* or *resistant*, which are promoted and sold in parallel ways to products that do not attempt to conceal their own origins in vulgar, conservative, capitalist consumerism. These *resistance* products are labeled in multiple ways in order to satisfy, reinforce, or even create tastes that are antithetical to the consumerist system. It might seem that these products are challenges to the market, but their credibility as antagonistic practices is neutralized by the power of a trendy and profitable cannibalization orchestrated by the contemporary market.

Thus, it is not difficult to find *alternative* options available on the market labeled as "political action" or "critique." Market logics can transform any kind of resistance into an exploitable market niche; everything can become an object of consumption. Given these favorable conditions for the creation of market niches and the growing demand for products and services associated with gore capitalism, what becomes possible is the creation of a market niche we call the *gore marketplace*. In this marketplace, the products and services offered are those associated with necropower and necropractices, that is, the sale of illegal drugs, violent activities, the sale of human organs, murder, trafficking of women and children, et cetera. The fact that everything can be absorbed by the market to create a niche and a demand does not mean that this absorption is *immediate*. This opens the possibility of taking oppositional action or undertaking critical resistance to this state of affairs. We nonetheless have to constantly reimagine the form of our resistance to the market. We should not begin with a simplistic or antagonistic position in relation to the market, but rather must keep in mind that subversion begins with a reformulation of our theories about practices of resistance and consumption so that we can reconsider the phenomenon as a whole, while distancing ourselves from a dichotomous vision.

We have to cease to see "pure" and direct resistance as the only possible strategy; we should bank on a reformulation linked to and situated within the context of the *bioeconomy* as a frame that both contains us and exceeds us. We might begin to subvert this frame through our *strategic relations*, which as Foucault argues, "being power games, ended up being infinitesimal, mobile, reversible, unstable."[4] This is due to the fact that in the face of market logics and the speed of contemporary life, certain interpretive categories no longer hold up as valid, solid and without flaws, but rather are categories in need of updating. To continue to cling tightly to the "desire for purification of what is thinkable is in and of itself an aporia."[5]

We construct categories that are contaminated and hybridized by other contemporary languages used to theorize reality; these categories are multidisciplinary and intersectional, and they speak to us of the possibility for reticular enunciation. Within these categories, bodies do not lose political density. Undeniably, these are bio-artifactual categories that help us to think and to resist, without renouncing our position, actions and responsibility in the reality of the *biomarket* and of gore capitalism.

What Third World discourses demonstrate is that, though we cannot evade the frame of this new form of capitalism, we can gain strength from understanding that this sole option—with its multiple labels and infinite possibilities—must not annihilate us, but rather re-signify us. Our position should not be resignation in the face of this maelstrom, but rather to re-signify ourselves and to interweave discourses of resistance, cognizant of the capitalist context within which these discourses have arisen and within which they will continue to develop as a kind of molecular subversion, since the *biomarket* is an introjected condition more than a choice.

The market plays an enormous role in the category of spectrality, as Baudrillard noted in his *For a Critique of the Political Economy of the Sign* that would later become his theory of the simulacrum. As Derrida has pointed out in his essays about spectrographies, the market also becomes a category for reinterpretation of the devices that, through mass media, come to define and give shape to ways of looking. Thus, our proposal to recodify the market as *biomarket* does not deny the possibility for real action and for jamming contemporary reality as it is affected discursively and actively by consumerist suppositions; rather, we are investigating another one of the discursive levels that contribute to and sustain the flourishing of gore capitalism.

Decorative Violence

In Madrid (a city belonging to the European Union, with everything that that implies), it would seem inconceivable to find a store window displaying an AK-47[6] that has been refashioned into a lamp, sold as the most of-the-moment and trendy way to show solidarity with the Third World. And yet, this store window exists,[7] and this lamp is one of the products offered by a lighting store called Oliva, located at 64 Calle Hortaleza in the central part of the city. In this store, these *weapon-lamps* are on display and for sale; prices range from 900 to 1,300 euros. There is an attempt to justify their sale as an act of solidarity, since 10% of the sale is to be donated to support the work of Doctors Without Borders.

It seems paradoxical that a weapon that has been used to kill millions of people around the world would be the object selected to marshal support for Doctors Without Borders (despite the respectable contribution and assistance they provide to the Third World). This is a serious blow to the Western conception of humanism. The sale of decorative violence is becoming ever more popular in European cities. This is a trend that has been apparent for decades in the United States, where annual conventions are held around the country to sell arms of all types to civilians, who justify their purchases as *personal defense* or *gun collecting*.

Witnessing consumption of this sort, we cannot help but think that what we are seeing is the crystallization and direct legitimization of gore consumption. What we are seeing is also the irresponsible and acritical acceptance of violence as a decorative element. The fact that violence has become *decorative* should seriously trouble us, since it provides an indication of the calculated implementation of gore epistemology. Its attendant creation of categories of interpretation and its derealized, aseptic, and utterly dystopian approach to the world contrasts with the true function of violence in our contemporary societies. If we ground our solidarity with the exploited in the consumption of decorative violence, what that says about us is that we are active participants in the problem of violence.

Gore consumption also demonstrates the power of the market to make everything consumable, but above all it shows the consumption practices that reflect a desire for destruction in affluent First World societies. Or, in the words of Angélica Liddell:

Now that you live with complete security,
now that you have rid yourselves of all your enemies,

finally, of all your enemies,

now,

you have no idea how to handle your weakness,

your lust for suffering,

your guilt,

your desires,

your meanness

and your insults.

After the massacre is over, the question becomes:

what does man do to continue to show,

to show himself,

that he is still a man? (Liddell, 2007, 38)

A kalashnikov as a decorative object in public (home decor stores) and private spaces in European cities exemplifies how globalization collapses distances and effaces differences in a perverse and dehumanizing way. That someone can purchase the most widely used killing machine in the world in order to demonstrate their solidarity seems particularly gruesome. This surrendering to total consumption is inexorably aligned with (and contributes to) the dominion of gore capitalism. What is obtained in exchange is a symbolic recognition of social status. Or as Saviano explains it:

The AK-47 ... has been the prop for every role: liberator, oppressor, soldier, terrorist, robber, and the special forces who guard presidents. [The] Kalashnikov … is the true symbol of free enterprise. The absolute icon. It can become the emblem of anything: it doesn't matter who you are, what you think, where you come from, what your religion is, who you're for, or what you're against, as long as you do what you do using our product. (Saviano, 2008, 177–8)

Both *gore consumption* and *the aesthetics of violence* or *decorative violence* expose that in the general consumerist imaginary, the sole way to demonstrate recognizable, praiseworthy, acceptable, and viable solidarity, empathy, critique, or resistance within gore capitalism is through consumption. They also expose a paradigm shift in the arms race that the majority of First World countries engage in: selling arms to less-privileged countries enabling them to wage their civil wars. This paradigm shift could be said to be founded on the idea that *if you are not using weapons to kill, use them to decorate.*

Understanding violence as decorative psychologically prepares society, making violence progressively less offensive, dangerous, and frightening, allowing both public and private spaces to be invaded by consumption with clear connections to warfare, ultimately converting these objects into desirable, enjoyable, and consumable items.

Another example of objects with clear connections to warfare are the all-terrain vehicles known as Hummers,[8] which have been widely accepted by consumers. These vehicles were manufactured by the U.S. company General Motors. The militaristic aesthetic of these vehicles is intentional: they are modeled on the Humvee or HMMWV (High Mobility Multipurpose Wheeled Vehicle), a multiuse military vehicle with four-wheel drive. Originally manufactured by the AM General Corporation, the former motor vehicle division of the U.S. government and armed forces, this same company decided to begin to sell vehicles to civilians at the end of the 1980s.

Our ever-increasing consumption of decorative violence is evidence that the demands of the *biomarket* have made us believe it is desirable for the contemporary world to reproduce the scenography of war. This leads to intellectual paralysis and an acritical outlook that fails to question the serious implications of war-related consumption and decorative violence in our daily lives. These practices further displace humanist suppositions and expand the scope of violence considered permissible; they also naturalize the indiscriminate use of violence through the participation-consumption of it by everyday citizens. This legitimates this system and its ties to violence, normalizing violence itself by proffering it simply as another product for consumption. The immediate consequence is that we put out the welcome mat for the arrival of gore capitalism, allowing it to occupy our public spaces, private spaces, and our very bodies.

On Violence and the Media

"The public will be created on the condition that certain images do not appear in the media, certain names of the dead are not utterable, certain losses are not avowed as losses, and violence is derealized and diffused" (Butler, 2006, 37–8). Information is power wielded in the service of the winner, and the media function as *news-washers* who prepare minds for all traces of dissidence to be eradicated: tools for the suppression of all dissent, even internal. The media function as over-expositors of violence, which they naturalize for viewers through a constant bombardment of images to the point where they turn violence itself into a kind of *manifest destiny*, to which we can only think to resign ourselves.

What the media enacts are exclusionary logics and practices of erasure. As Virginia Villaplana has argued: "It is essential to name the forms of violence and to continue to work on symbolic violence—what is not named does not exist—so that these are not reduced to individual experiences and/or accidents and to put them into a social and critical context" (Villaplana & Sichel, 2005, 279).

The lack of discourse that might attempt to name what is happening in the Other world is perpetuated by the media's "overrepresentation…from one sole point of view" (Villaplana & Sichel, 2005, 279). The media legitimates only that which seems "familiar," stories that "I understand" and "I can relate to." Yet, what happens when this "familiarity" or "relatability" are out of reach or when the stories do not include me at all? What is my role as a viewer in the face of the naturalization of violence perpetuated in the media? What is my responsibility in the face of my own consumption of gore images?

The growing reification of violence in contemporary societies (acritically accepted and naturalized as a normal occurrence) has meant that for a long time the rise of gore practices has gone unnoticed. These practices are seen as part of an alternate reality, part of "a thing that happened far away, that affected prices and supplied the newspapers with exciting headlines and pictures. [Violence seen] through an iridescent mist, deodorized, scented indeed, with all its essential cruelties tactfully hidden away" (Davis, 2002, 1). Now these practices have emerged as an unstoppable force, fused with daily life.

The interweaving of reality and simulacrum has progressed in such a way that it is increasingly harder (or we have been made to believe as much) to distinguish between reality and fiction, since "the more improbable the event, the more familiar the image" (Davis, 2002, 5).

The news media and the entertainment industry (*mass media* in general) have drowned us in information and have wrought havoc on our ability to perceive, accept, and act in reality. Capitalism and its production of gore imagery has crossed over the strange, thin line between fantasy and reality, producing a complete reversal that re-establishes reality as something horrifying and true that increasingly resembles fiction, but differs from fiction in that it is heartbreakingly palpable and irreparable. This is because, despite the production of media images that attempt to fictionalize what is real, what we see is an argument for *non-fiction*. (Villaplana y Sichel, 2005, 279).

This new capitalism[9] appears frightening because it means that anything can happen—and in fact does happen—and in the most intimate arena: in the body itself. Gore practices horrify us because they are closer and closer to us and we have not been taught how to think about them, and even less so to confront them. "The problem is that no one can afford to think he's not involved. It's not enough to assume that the way you live your life will protect you from every danger" (Saviano, 2008, 91). This unleashes an *interminable uncanny effect*[10] that violently undermines our ontologies and erases the distinction between imagination and reality. It unleashes the sensation of being inside a house of mirrors in which the uncanny repeats and multiplies before our eyes without us ever knowing which of the images is real, or if all of them are. In this respect, some theorists have asked: has history simply become a mad montage of prefabricated horrors crafted in Hollywood writers' rooms? (Davis, 2002, 5). The answer is yes and no, since this *dark utopia* is in fact more complex (Bloch, 2004, 306–8).

This question can elicit suspicion and derision—laughter gives us a momentary break from fear—and lead us to believe that contemporary reality can be read as a montage attempting to reproduce the unreal. Reality comes to symbolize the fact that "the ultimate truth of the capitalist utilitarian de-spiritualized universe is the de-materialization of 'real life' itself, its reversal into spectral show" (Žižek, 2005, 128). Nevertheless, this reading—though it is largely applicable to reality—leads us to make abstract theorizations that merely duplicate or explain it from a post-materialist theoretical position unconnected to real practices and their consequences that intervene in and transform subjects and societies.

In addition, we have to accept that gore practices have been forged within a concrete history as a direct response to specific market demands. We must take into account that violence as a tool is an integral part of the message transmitted by this new capitalism; violence is one of the methods for acquiring capital, and it is used to further perpetuate the ruthless pursuit of money. It is also important to consider that, though endriago subjects in many instances belong to distinct contexts and are disseminated across the planet, none of them is exempted from the effects of information overload.

We have to take into account that it is the media, television, film, and—to a greater or lesser degree—videogames that depict these practices as derealized (if not fictional) phenomena.[11] They legitimate these practices by making them their central theme and incessantly bombarding us with information about them to the point of desensitization.

Death is in Style: Gore Capitalism in Art, Literature and Video Games

In this section, we will provide some examples of the imaginaries that are built and distributed through the media and that we have identified in this book as depictions of gore capitalism. The first example is the television series *The Sopranos* and the second is the video game *Grand Theft Auto: San Andreas*.

The Sopranos is a U.S. televisions series directed by David Chase and produced by HBO that focused on the life of an Italian-American[12] mafia boss in New Jersey and his family. It is not insignificant that it was one of the most critically-acclaimed series of its time, winning significant awards and garnering a huge fan base, including several well-known intellectuals (De los Ríos, et al (2009). The series was remarkably long-lasting— due to the lurid nature of the topic—and was broadcast from 1999 through 2007.

This series is a clear example of how television has made the underworld into something profitable, glorifying it as a cult object and elevating it for acceptance and legitimacy. We are not arguing that the creation of series like this one has in and of itself built the framework for gore practices to jump from the screen to reality and to establish themselves within capitalism, with hardly a word or complaint from the public. What we are positing is that series like these are one way to make visible and to legitimate violence, mentally preparing the public to passively engage with reality around them. That is, gore capitalism was already rooted in daily life; what the media seeks to do is legitimate its existence and impede actions by society to counter it. The media attempts to encourage an acritical, resigned, and silent position in the face of these phenomena. By presenting the reality of gore capitalism in a television series or a reality show (which many people would want to participate in), the media makes it troublingly glamorous, desirable, and consumable. This removes any sense of real danger and shapes consciousness and behavior to desensitize people to its presence, especially since its consequences are rarely depicted.

Acclimating the public to the violence of gore capitalism benefits the gore capitalist system on a number of different levels: one of the most obvious is the displacement of ethical and political directives. That is, the introduction and legitimation of a social imaginary in which violence and crime have become mere tools for earning money means that any criminal behavior (above all when carried out by governmental actors) is perfectly acceptable. This hinders the ability of ethics to aid us in addressing certain phenomena and lets quasi-illegal political practices off the hook, since criminality is understood as a tool that abides by standards established by global economic leaders.

We also want to mention the videogame *Grand Theft Auto* as another example of gore capitalism, since the game's violent contents allow players to commit criminal acts varying from car theft to homicide. It legitimates behaviors that are profoundly male-chauvinist, sexist,[13] misogynist and violent towards women; for example, in the game, *it's possible to have sex with a prostitute and then kill her to get your money back*. Nonetheless, we are not mentioning this in order to register our complaints as victims, but rather to use the videogame and its contents to show two of the interconnected poles that represent, from our perspective, the principal strands of the birth, rise, and ongoing dominance of gore capitalism.

First, the game shows the criminals (who we define in this project as endriago subjects) as part of a consumerist culture and as a direct response to a system (in the U.S.) that perpetuates horrible social inequalities and, in addition, openly celebrates them:

Here's a good example of one of the satirical commercials heard on the radio stations of San Andreas. The ad is promoting author Mike Andrew's speaking tour in which he tries to convince people that, as his book's title puts it, *Rags Are Riches*:

MIKE ANDREWS: "Understand that it's okay to be poor. There needs to be poor people. We rich are the yin. You are the yang. We need you!"

MAN FROM AUDIENCE: "Mr Andrews, I've had a run of bad luck and I was wondering if the state could help me get back on my feet?"

ANDREWS: "This is the negative kind of self-obsessed greedy talk that doesn't help anyone. My program will teach you a new outlook on life. Instead of complaining about being poor, enjoy it. Watch TV. Don't vote. Who cares?"

MAN: "But I'm homeless."

ANDREWS: "You've got it all wrong. Society doesn't owe you anything. The government has better things to worry about, like killing innocent people. You already have everything you need, so enjoy your lives." (Lavigne, 2005)

This videogame portrays the use of violence as an everyday practice that is embedded in a social framework founded on explicit violence. Thus, commercials like this one emerge in a specific context and

… position the crimes and violence perpetrated by your character … against a background of increasing disparity between rich and poor as well as government-sponsored violence against foreign populations. San Andreas takes place during the early 1990s, a time when President George H.W. Bush was furthering the neo-conservative economic and social policies started under Ronald Reagan and the United States had just finished launching military attacks against Panama and Iraq while maintaining a bloody "war on drugs" in Latin America. (Lavigne, 2005)

What is revealed are the structures and contexts from which endriago subjects have emerged, at the same time as the game shows us the direct connections between these subjects and systems understood as legal and their governments. The links between the world of crime and the world of the State are made clear:

> … as CJ finds himself taking orders from a government agent involved in "battling threats in Latin America by any means necessary." This agent's methods include trading and dealing drugs to raise money for "overseas interests" as well as "financing militaristic dictators in exchange for arms contracts." And while the government's tactics are highly illegal, the agent justifies them as the only way to protect the United States and, specifically, its capitalist culture. (Lavigne, 2005)

Secondly, the game illustrates in a parodic way how both the media and the government (and its representatives) are controlled by corporate interests. Thus we find evidence of how the media is interconnected with the State and obeys direct orders from it in order to skew the information that is broadcast to the public, buttressing consumerist, acritical and silent imagos.

An example of this connection is found in the station ads for WCTR, one of many radio stations found in the videogame. In these ads, the news channel identifies itself as broadcasting "all the news the government wants you to hear" or as purveyors of "everything to make you feel manly and patriotic" and whose slogan, approved by Rupert Murdoch[14] is "we distort, you can't retort" (Lavigne, 2005). It should be clear that this videogame is a trenchant critique of a system that can be understood as pure gore capitalism.

However, we cannot ignore the debate that has arisen about the accessibility and interpretation of the game's critique, and whether it is actually clear and can be understood by the majority of the people playing it. There is a possibility that the players are left with a flat image that glorifies violence, or even that the game incites them to use it as a means of empowerment. The argument is that the game cannot be read as critique by those players who lack discursive referents, whether due to their age or their education.[15]

We do not want to overlook the psychologists who have argued that games which require active use of violence can channel aggressiveness, becoming a means to discharge destructive impulses without them being carried out in reality. Our position with respect to violent videogames does not attempt to satanize or condemn them, but instead proposes a critical reading of the information they provide. In any case, what is quite clear is that *Grand Theft Auto*—which can be played from the comfort of one's home—is the virtual crystallization of what we have classified as gore capitalism.

Let's return here to the importance of media in creating, transmitting, and legitimating the system for interpreting or de-codifying reality. In our view, this makes it entirely relevant to speak of indirect feedback between the media and endriago subjects. That is, the circulation and sensationalization of violence informs the endriagos about the criminal tools and methods to employ in their execution and performance of criminal tasks, as well as the results of these tasks and the social significance of each illegal act. The media even educates them about the "popularity," "profitability," and the degree of risk that each crime carries with it.

Information in Hollywood movies could serve as a user's manual for the practices of gore capitalism; each criminal act that is televised and retransmitted to society serves as feedback teaching endriago subjects strategies to increase the efficacy of their practices. We should not ignore that the criminals who belong to new mafia structures have been educated in and with the logics of spectacle: they know how to work a stage; they know how to manipulate screens and newspapers; they know how to use electronic media and pirate radio stations; they know how to post videos of their killings online, accessible to everyone. That is, they know that "spectacle is superior to enigmatic codes of winking or the well-defined mythology of infamous crime neighborhoods" (Saviano, 2008, 111).

Just as endriago subjects are not outside the reach of the media, the rest of our social fabric is not far from gore. It is symptomatic of this that it is in art, literature, and journalism, rather than in philosophy, where we find the first accounts of the practices of gore capitalism. There are an ever growing number of literary authors who decry the expansion of organized crime, that is, who expose the dangerous mix of mafias, corruption, religion, machismo, and exploitation.

An example of a writer doing critical work on the mafia is the Italian Massimo Carlotto, who unpacks the myth of the Italian mafia's aura and argues that, "the myth of the criminality of the good family man who takes care of his family on the weekends is an utter lie. [Italy] is incredibly violent and lives its strange perversion of justice 24 hours a day, seven days a week" (Mora, 2008). This mention of Italy is interesting, since it has long been a reference point when talking about organized crime, and we mention it here as a criminal enclave in regions outside of the Third World.

Carlotto also discusses the qualitative change that has taken place within the internal networks of the mafia. He tells us that in Italy "the lowest level is occupied by the Albanians who are known for their participation in prostitution in Venice, while the highest position is held by the economic criminals who disguise themselves as honorable citizens and are protected by local and regional politicians" (Mora, 2008). It seems important to state clearly that criminal practices in a variety of contexts are linked to corrupt governments and protected by them. It is no secret that mafias have infiltrated all economic sectors. It is no secret either that mafias have spread their reach into all levels of society, and that they have relationships and partners everywhere.

Another undeniable fact—which is hardly mentioned—is the high level of corruption that exists in certain States. This cover-up means that the underworld engages directly and substantially in criminal activities, yet it is difficult to track and punish.

The influence of gore capitalism leads to a discursive turn that founds a new gore narrative, which expands dramatically at all levels of society, including within art. This discourse has been crystallized ever more forcefully in the work of hundreds of contemporary artists. Examples of this work can be found with visual artists like Teresa Margolles (Mexico, 1963), who has worked since the 1990s with fluids, organs, and human corpses. Another example is Doctor Lacra (Mexico,

1972) whose work focuses on marginality, and who said regarding death as a trend: "Fifteen years ago, Santa Muerte[16] was a religious icon venerated exclusively by criminals and prostitutes, but now she is in style" (Espinosa, 2008).

Thus, in the realm of art, death is another "fashion trend omnipresent on the street, and it is already boring" (Espinosa, 2008). This is not strange in a society in which extreme violence and death have become fashionable objects of consumption, which once adapted to commercial logics must be *reinvented* in order to continue flourishing in the market.

There is a segment of the art world that is quite critical of the rise of death as fashion and actively condemns its potential causes and consequences. Mellanie Pullen is a New York photographer who uses her images to think through the double standard used to encode death in today's world. As she has commented, "Movies have become so violent and the commercialization of news and lurid images is so palpable that they have had a profound effect on people. My work decries precisely that spectralization of death through drama, of its theatricalized reproduction" (Espinosa, 2008).

We can see that both spectralization and derealization are strategies the system uses to create psychological mechanisms that legitimate the use of violence. Violence as a tool is not used exclusively by endriago subjects, but rather also by the system which, as it becomes increasingly incapable of providing for the welfare of its citizens, concurrently and paradoxically becomes more and more repressive, demanding the creation of categories to justify, legitimate, and absolve it of any responsibility for this repression. We will reflect more on this point in the following pages, grounding our thinking on the suppositions of Judith Butler in regard to the precariousness of life, both on an economic level but also discursively and existentially.

Addendum: *Derealization and Spectralization*

In this section, we posit the term derealization[17] as a strategy that defines the discourse that looks to declare the Third World a derealized world. This concept retains colonialist stripes and is continually reaffirmed by its use in the media. This derealization or spectralization in the media is imposed as a filter for a discomfiting reality, what Judith Butler has written about as a way of *othering*, foreignizing, removing something from the context of the known to create a sense of alienation and distance that is both symbolic and emotional in the receiver. The result is that the derealized subject or context is made illegitimate.

The derealization imposed by dominant media discourse ends up being the only valid way for those who manage and transmit information to refer to peripheral and impoverished spaces. Business and State policies are also built on the foundation laid by this derealization; these entities have exchanged the strategy of silence for one based on distortion and information overload, which leads to the derealization of the phenomenon or subject in question.

First, derealization attacks the concept of the Third World itself, designating it as politically incorrect and arguing that the term has no place in contemporary discourse because it is not applicable to current conditions. This move circumvents the use of this concept, relegating it to an arena that makes it seem indecent. In this way, it also thwarts any possibility of articulating a discourse that might lead to agency and empowerment for subjects whose daily lives take place in Third World territories. This denial of discourse and agency has a derealizing effect on these subjects, depicting them as silent, inarticulate, and ineffectual.

It is essential that the concept of spectralization not be reduced to the dissolution of the Other and for it also to play a crucial role in contemporary economic logics. On the one hand, this is the preferred formula for denying uncomfortable realities and maintaining the bubble produced by the media, insofar as it has to do with the spectralization

of the Third World. Nevertheless, this spectralization, which is best represented in *virtual capital*,
must be refuted as a category for interpreting
reality, because the deaths of the people destroyed
by this capital are real. Death is never virtual for
the people who lose their lives.

On the other hand, spectralization is used to
conceal—and to exempt from responsibility—the
governments, corporations and, more generally,
the entire system undergirding contemporary gore
capitalism. Through spectralization, the idea has
been disseminated that the system is unstoppable,
diffuse, and beyond the control of any one subject,
government, or corporation; in the face of this
system, we find ourselves in a state of immutable
helplessness.

However, we must refute the argument that the
market is a self-directed, unfettered, and unfathomable phenomenon, since it can better understood
as a well-organized, highly-managed phenomenon,
steeped in the logics of the new Darwinist, ultracapitalist right wing. We could say that the market
is a highly-organized structure, regulated and
managed by specific subjects—who can be held
accountable—since "the market needs rules and
these rules have to be instituted by someone. There
are authorities who produce, supervise and, natu-
rally, make sure that these regulations are effective"
(Estévez & Taibo, 2008, 54). Definitely, we must

keep in mind that the market has rules and directors. As Negri argues:

> Today we are living through an interregnum between modernity and postmodernity, between the age of the nation-state and the age of empire, and in this interlude struggles are developing with the aim of finding some balance in capitalist relations and also in military relations, that is, in the relations of power. (Estévez & Taibo, 2008, 54).

It is precisely in this interregnum where the role of gore practices becomes essential, since they are an indissoluble part of the contemporary capitalism system. Capital derived from organized crime—about fifteen percent of worldwide GDP[18]—is so entirely fused with capital from transnational corporations and global capital that it is practically unthinkable to imagine the contemporary economy without the financial contributions of organized crime.

For this reason, gore capitalism is one of the central axes for the interpretation of contemporary reality, since it makes its presence felt across multiple domains and is a fundamental part of the economy in all sectors. This means that it is difficult to posit axes for effective interpretation without taking into account distinct variations and working across disciplinary boundaries. Thus, in our view, gore capitalism is a foundational and interdisciplinary concept for economic and philosophical analysis of our contemporary world. Originally linked to the film genre that gave it its name, gore makes certain forms of representation visible through an over-depiction of excessively cruel violence, making that violence an anecdotal and even comical action, thus provoking cognitive dissonance between the images of extreme violence and the paradoxical depiction of these actions in a cynical way, bordering on obscenity. However, at the same time, gore impedes the articulation of arguments that might confront this cognitive dissonance and its implications, thus leading to the acritical acceptance of the most recalcitrant violence applied against bodies. This violence is one of the key characteristics of contemporary capitalism, which has posited itself as the sole option for the world since the end of the 1980s. Its dominion prevails no matter the government or political movement.

In this book, we have condemned the fact that capitalism has been established as the only global economic option, which has reinforced its supposed status as the only viable path for developing an economic project. We think it necessary to analyze this phenomenon through a wider lens than just the demonization of capitalism; we think it necessary to pursue an analysis with other non-binary methods, without, of course, exempting capitalism from its responsibility in the contemporary transformation of the world and the direct consequences in the growing inequality that is leading to the outbreak of rampant violence as a practice of capitalism. We understand the exercise of violence primarily in the sense of its direct and physical application to bodies, though we do also consider it in its other modes of symbolic or media violence.

We are entirely in agreement with statements made by Beneyto about the need for the left to craft a new socioeconomic alternative. It is time to leave behind the post-traumatic syndrome that has plagued the left since the collapse of the Soviet system. We must return to the ethical values of the left to redirect political and social actions, with the goal of creating new alliances and coalitions with other non-dystopian political practices.

We have to fight against the entrenched idea that crime pays, in other words, that violence and criminality are extremely profitable economic processes—even though in fact they are. We need to establish restrictions to allow for a more peaceful coexistence and emphasize the right to not be a victim of predatory violence in the pursuit of economic enrichment.

This transformation must occur through education at all levels, and principally through language, since we do everything with words; we need to bestow words with precise meanings in order to achieve "a minimum level of historical, ideological, and terminological coherence" (Estévez & Taibo, 2008, 91). If we do not, it will lead us to a further displacement between signifiers and signifieds and to the effective loss of actions articulated in language. We should not forget the performative nature of language, which allows it to simultaneously create the reality it articulates. Articulating in a different way is, in some sense, a way of redirecting the reality that has been imposed on us through dystopian practices and discourses.

5

At the Brink of El Bordo, I Become Blade:
Gore Capitalism and Feminism(s)

> The foundation for a future politics of social transforma-
> tion and rupture are the very processes of subjectification
> and singularization that are opposed to modes of domina-
> tion; these processes would have to allow for the permanent
> reinvention of ways of being and of words.
>
> —Virginia Villaplana. *Zonas de Intensidades*
> *[Zones of Intensities]*

Throughout this book, we have examined how the
heightened technification and rationalization of
violence as a tool for the production of wealth has
put life and the body—as a container for the former—at the core of gore capitalism. We believe it
is also critical to link this topic with feminism as
both political practice and epistemological category in order to posit new axes of resistance that
might redirect or subvert gore capitalism's endriago
subjectivities, which are rooted in *marginalized*

masculinity (Helfrich, 2001, 233). This *marginalized masculinity* is found in "men who are part of subordinated social classes or ethnic groups ... who also help to sustain the power of hegemonic masculinity, because they interiorize the structural elements of its practices" (Helfrich, 2001, 233). This form of masculinity is based on obedience to hegemonic, capitalist, and heteropatriarchal masculinity; it thereby attempts to legitimate itself and to advance hegemonic power, seeing dissidence as purely dystopian and violent. This makes these men unable to question the assumptions of the system as it is imposed on them in the name of power, economics, and masculinity.

For several decades, it has been clear that feminism is not singular, but rather its movements are comparable to a single drop of mercury that bursts and becomes many, yet preserves the ability to multiply, separate, and re-attach through alliances. As a movement guided by a critique of both oppression and the violence of a hegemonic, (hetero)patriarchal system, it would be impossible for feminist discourse not to theorize or take actions against the dynamics of gore capitalism. From our multiple and distinct feminist positions, it is urgent to situate ourselves in a critical posture vis-à-vis this system. We need to be open to internally-focused criticality and redefinition in order to confront the variety of issues of concern to both first feminisms and to new feminisms and post-feminisms rooted in the specific contexts of our contemporary realities. These realities have their own subtleties and particularities, and yet they are all impacted by the physical, psychological, and mass-media ramifications of the increasing globalization of gore violence and its very real effects on gender. Gore capitalism nurtures and artificially naturalizes a "deliberately fractured narrative strategy" (Villaplana & Sichel (2005), 269) that impacts all discursive fields and can be identified, with particular intensity, in how the media presents misogynist violence.

We do not claim that the categories of gore capitalism proposed in this investigation are identical in all contexts. However, violence as a tool for building wealth is increasingly found in distinct, geographically-separated spaces. It is being globalized and intertwined with the creation of subjectivities and agencies determined by capitalist forces of monitoring and production.

Women have lived in gore realities throughout history, as have those subjects understood as subaltern or dissident in relation to heteropatriarchal categories. Women have lived with extreme physical and psychological violence, and more recently with the additional violence transmitted through the media; these have been part of our daily lives and our education. Violence has been a core element in constructing a discourse (Bernárdez, 2001) that assumes that conditions of vulnerability and violence are women's *manifest destiny*,[1] something like an inverse privilege, "a stigma that forces us into a Russian roulette of barbarous creatures" (Liddell, 2008). This is why we are all invested in developing a cogent response to gore capitalism's fierce violence, as it affects a wide array of bodies that cannot be reduced to the rigid hierarchy of feminine and masculine.

The radical nature of this violence brings us to the brink, to the transformation of one age into another; this period requires us to analyze our inherited concepts, shake off our theories, and update them. The ferocity of gore capitalism leaves us with no other options besides the creation of new political subjects for feminism, that is, "a becoming-woman [understood as] any break with society's present mode of functioning" (Guattari & Rolnik, 2006, 113). We need to weave alliances with other minority becomings and rise together in response to "a 'phallocratic' mode of production of subjectivity—a politics of desire in which the accumulation of capital, prestige and power are the sole guiding principles" (Guattari & Rolnik, 2006, 112). It is in this space where we find the roots of the becoming-endriago and gore capitalism.

Today, in the centers of world power, feminism as a social movement has endured a critique that paints it as both obsolete and ahistorical, even within more progressive social movements that otherwise defend the creation of dissidence and resistance groups. This is an utter inconsistency since the society

> ... fiercely denounces social and racial injustice, but [is] indulgent and understanding when it comes to male domination. Many [men] try to explain that the feminist struggle is ancillary, a luxury sport of little relevance or urgency. You would have to be a moron, or else horribly dishonest, to think one oppression insufferable and another full of charm. (Despentes, 2010, 28)

Feminism is important in the world—whether in the First or Third Worlds—since women "earn less money than men, hold less senior posts, and are used to not being acknowledged" (Despentes, 2010, 20). We live in a world in which "capitalism is an egalitarian religion in the sense that it demands general submission, making everyone feel trapped—as all women are" (Despentes, 2010, 31). Contemporary capitalism has led us to a breakdown in the labor system as a result of the obscene radicalization of neoliberalism and the predatory transformation of the economic system.

It is worth noting that the capitalist system in its gore incarnation—which today is threatened by the necroempowerment of endriago subjects, who are mainly male—still neglects to take into account what we, as women, have to say about this new version of capitalism that is even more twisted, violent, and extreme.

It might seem strange to talk about female empowerment under the current framework of persistent violence. However, the undeniable fact of the capitalist, patriarchal system's fracturing and unsustainability open the door to feminisms and their associated practices in order to continue framing ways of being in the world that decenter heteropatriarchal capitalism's worldview. In other words, this epistemic break—to which capitalism in its most savage version has brought us—opens the door for us to rethink gore capitalism and, using feminist tools, to forge a new discourse and sustainable practices that will move us away from it.

Gore capitalism has unsettled many of the fundamental principles that undergird humanist discourse; one of them is that male subjects, just like the upper classes, are no longer untouchable in today's world. All of these previously respectable subjects have become fungible bodies susceptible to torture and eradication in order to produce further wealth.

It should be pointed out that although in some countries feminism has made concrete achievements—especially in Nordic countries and in

Spain—with juridical equality and laws defending women, in everyday terms feminism is still an urgent cause. This is because it represents a change in terms of epistemology and social consciousness that cannot be reduced to clichés or moderate achievements. We must understand that:

> Feminism is a revolution, not a rearranged marketing strategy, or some kind of promotion of fellatio or swinging; not just a matter of increasing secondary wages. Feminism is a collective adventure, for women, men, and everyone else. A revolution, well under way. A worldview. A choice. It's not a matter of contrasting women's small advantages with men's small assets, but of sending the whole lot flying. (Despentes, 2010, 146)

We want to stress that feminism is also for men, since the failure of masculinity in its *hegemonic, complicit, or marginalized* versions[2] inflicts an enormous symbolic and emotional cost on men and places them in extremely conflicted space. Hegemonic masculinity is dissociated from its relations with all others, regardless of their gender. Thus, we should remember that masculine-gendered identities are adaptable since "what manifests in a particular moment as a masculine-gendered identity is the result of a process of transformation. Characteristics defined as masculine ... must be questioned, because their meanings are solely results of a historical and social practice" (Botteher, 2005, 235). We must remember that gender identities are part of the *habitus* that has artificially naturalized them and created gendered social constructions of the world and the body, while converting perpetrators into victims (Bourdieu, 2002, 94).

In the light of the dissolution of previous economic structures, there is an attempt to construct new forms of intersubjective relations or of *alternative figurations of subjectivity* (Villaplana & Sichel, 2005, 271) that might help to change the direction of the devastating current reality, based as it is on a military-consumerist-patriarchal-gore-capitalist system.

Transfeminism and Gore Capitalism

Here at the critical juncture defined by gore capitalism, we see the emergence of *transfeminism*,[3] an articulation of both a system of thought and a form of social resistance that preserves certain feminist assertions regarding the acquisition of rights in geopolitically distinct spaces, while also integrating mobility between genders, corporalities, and sexualities. This mobility has aided in the creation of site-specific strategies identified with the Deleuzian idea of minorities, multiplicities, and singularities that together form a networked organization able to "unyieldingly reappropriate and intervene in the advocacy slogans of 'woman,' 'identity,' 'liberty' or 'equality,' in other words, to disseminate 'living revolutions'" (Preciado, 2009a).

The prefix *trans* refers to something that cuts through what it names, re-centering and transmuting it. When added to feminism(s), it creates a space of transit, a transhumance between ideas, a transformation that creates epistemological linkages. These linkages have micropolitical implications, understood as a process-oriented micropolitics focused on the acquisition of agency, through social fabric as it is formed and enters into contact with reality. What emerges is a counter-offensive working against "the social forces that administer capitalism today [who] understand that the production of subjectivity is possibly more important than any other kind of production, more essential than the production of petroleum and energy" (Guattari & Rolnick, 2008, 36).

Transfeminist subjects can be understood as *queer multitudes*, who through the performative materialization of their bodies are able to develop different kinds of g-local agency. These *queer multitudes* continue developing categories and enacting practices that result in non-standard agencies, not as an absolute truth nor as infallible actions, which can be applied in a variety of contexts in a deterritorialized way. These queer subjects play a critical role, given their conditions of intersectionality,[4] in the "confrontation between the ways that subjectivity is produced on a planetary scale" (Guattari & Rolnik, 2008, 40). It's crucial to make the causes and the consequences of physical violence visible, so that violence is not reduced to a media phenomenon where the problem is solely seen as "the battle for audience and the number of viewers achieved by the economic powers that uphold big media" (Bernárdez, 2001, 17). The treatment of violence in the media obscures the real problem, which is based on "the production and reproduction of violence against women [and against bodies in general] as a social phenomenon of discursive production [and production of wealth]" (Bernárdez, 2001, 9).

It's important to mention that "postcolonial, queer transfeminism is distinct from what Jacqui Alexander and Chandra Talpade Mohanty have called *free market feminism* that has taken on biopower's demands for surveillance and repression and demanded that censorship, punishment and criminalization be instituted in the name of and in order to protect women" (Preciado, 2009a). In contrast to *free market feminism*, transfeminism posits feminist discourses and practices that confront reality and are able to distance themselves from both political correctness—which demobilizes agency—and from *political window-dressing* enacted by purportedly-feminist institutions, which use these catchwords to conceal the most ferocious type of neoliberalism.

Practices of transfeminist agency are ways of furthering conversations posited by U.S. Third World feminism since the 1980s. This feminism has been led by intersectional, mestiza subjects like Chela Sandoval, Gloria Anzaldúa, Cherríe Moraga, and others. Sandoval especially has shown us the importance of re-interpretation, re-appropriation, and contextualization, in her case drawing on the work of Donna Haraway on cyborgs, technology, and hybrid species. This feminism has generated forms of agency and resistance within the same context that denies us space and shuts us down. As the members of the collective La Eskalera Karakola write in their prologue to *Otras inapropiables* [Unappropriatable Others]:[5]

Chela Sandoval argues for the practice of a U.S. Third World feminism that centers a differential, oppositional cyborg consciousness capable of generating forms of agency and resistance through oppositional technologies of power. For this author, the conditions that gave rise to cyborgs are associated with labor precarity, and workplace exploitation is linked to the technology that has given rise to Third World sections of the First World... (hooks, et al., 12)

Transfeminism incorporates an awareness of historical memory backed by the legacy of the feminist movements of the last two centuries, alongside a call to elaborate new theorizations of reality and the condition of women. In fact, these new theories would not only encompass women, but also the distinct corporalities and forms of dissidence that develop at the same speed and rhythm as contemporary reality. These theories also need to take into account the specific economic circumstances faced by subjects within the international labor (and existential) precariat.

In the context of the aforementioned global situation, it is notable that initiatives to create politico-social networks have not multiplied and that inter-gender alliances are not more prevalent as attempts to confront the devastating system of hyperconsumerist, gore capitalism. There is a specific reason for this: the patriarchal fear of loss of privileges, loss of power, or what is euphemistically called *the fear of the devirilization* of society. All of the linkages and assemblages that attempt to critique and marshal resistance to the dominant system must include an awareness of *becoming-woman*, *becoming-black*, *becoming-Indian*, *becoming-migrant*, *becoming-precarious*, rather than reifying their belonging to a sole gender or a social group and confining themselves to a turf battle. We must work on building a resistance that is a process in relation to other minoritarian processes, because resistance:

> …cannot appear in an isolated way disregarding all other social injustices and forms of discrimination. Rather the struggle … is only possible and truly effective within a constellation of conjoined struggles in solidarity against all other forms of oppression, marginalization, persecution, and discrimination. (Vidarte, 2007, 169)

It is possible to overcome the (masculinist) fear of losing *proprietary rights* over the system of powers and privileges called *masculinity* through a process that makes it clear that so-called masculine characteristics do not exclusively belong to male subjects, but rather they can be appropriated by any subject, regardless of their gender or sexual orientation. In addition, this process must also make it clear that the privileges offered as a reward for constant obedience to hegemonic masculinity are a risky investment. This investment charges large amounts of interest; on a material level, it also demands as payment that men become the objects of this predatory destruction affecting all bodies, not just the bodies of Others.

For this reason, despite similarities and differences in our ways of thinking, we see it as critical to de-center the category of masculinity, understood as an intrinsic and exclusive property of male bodies. This de-centering would lead to a discursive, non-violent reconstruction able to multiply the array of possibilities for the construction of new subjectivities, both for women and men. Included in these new categorizations would be both ciswomen and cismen as well as transwomen, transmen and all those who critically unsubscribe from gender dichotomies, creating a framework that expands our possibilities for action and recognition. The displacement of "certain attributes long defined as masculine, [like] skill, strength, speed, physical dominance [and] uninhibited use of space and motion" would lead to an unprecedented epistemological and discursive shift (Cahn, 1994, 279).

We know it is possible to unseat masculinity from its position in the gender hierarchy because it is a modifiable performative process on the part of men. This modification is imminent now that the capitalist world has become even more cruel and radically brutal, demanding that the surplus value of a product derive from bloodshed; right now, this system

> ... fails to meet the needs of men [and when it does, it exacts a higher and higher price for it]— no more work, loss of dignity at work, absurdity and cruelty of economic constraints, administrative irritations, bureaucratic humiliations, knowing

you'll be ripped off whenever you try to buy
something, [escalating violence]. (Despentes,
2010, 140)

In this context, it becomes urgent to analyze and reformulate the demands of hegemonic masculinity as they are transmitted by systems of domination that, in this book, we have linked to gore capitalism. There is a clear parallel between gore capitalism and hegemonic masculinity, which is "comprised of a constellation of values, beliefs, attitudes and behaviors that powerful authorities pursue in relation to people they consider weak" (Varela, 2005, 322).

It is simply not possible to build real resistance to the economic system in which we live—this system that bases its power on extreme violence—without questioning masculinity. This same masculinity also mutates into real violence enacted upon the bodies of men themselves. As José Ángel Lozoya writes, "expectations from adults, competition between guys, the authoritarianism of gangs, and the need instigated within them to prove to themselves and to others that they are, at the very least, as manly as the manliest among them lead men to take on unhealthy habits and reckless behaviors. These provoke a multiplicity of injuries, sicknesses and deaths, beginning in childhood" (Lozoya, 2002).

Transfeminism and New Masculinities

Transfeminism's creation of new political subjects re-opens the conversation about the need, relevance, and inherent challenges implied by masculine subjects positing new configurations and conditions for constructing masculinities that are capable not only of enacting but also of creating a discourse of resistance through them.[6]

The theoretical and practical construction of new masculinities must take gender and deconstruction into account. This work should also make use of the conceptual tools developed by feminisms that have reconsidered the feminine subject and decentered it by moving it toward forms that are non-hegemonic and not predetermined by biology.

As Simone de Beauvoir said, "One is not born, but rather becomes, a woman." Once again, this statement needs to be applied within the field of masculinity in order to decenter it and to develop constructions of masculinity that are grounded in lived reality and the embodiment of individual masculinities that demonstrate how one is not born a man either, but rather becomes one through an always-malleable process.

It is widely accepted that individuals with power and legitimacy will not easily give up those privileges. Nonetheless, the silent comfort which allows for the development of *complicit masculinities* must be called into question. Building off the work of Robert Connell, Martha Zapata Galindo defines complicit masculinity as that which

> characterizes men who do not defend the hegemonic prototype in a militant way, but who still are recipients of *patriarchal dividends*, that is they enjoy all of the advantages obtained as a result of discrimination against women. They benefit from material advantages, from prestige and authority without having to strain. (Böttcher, 2005, 233)

Thus, it is urgent and extremely important that while men deconstruct the model of hegemonic masculinity—which constrains the large majority of both women and men—they also need to end their silent passivity. In this respect, we need to clarify that there are many masculine subjects who want to, attempt to, and need to extricate themselves from these archaic and oppressive patterns, but who also report that this process of extrication or gender disobedience is hardly an easy task. As Luis Bonino argues,

> The fears and mistrust of some men in the face of so much *newness* deter them from change. Additional deterrents are the lack of models for non-traditional masculinity and the silent isolation of men allied with women, since they often are ashamed to speak publicly about their

> alliances. The condemnation of men who trans-
> gress traditional gender norms is also very effec-
> tive, since men are concerned about the opinions
> of their peers. (Lomas, 2003), 127)

Despite the costs incurred by renouncing traditional masculinity, it is urgent to do so because this
will allow for the planning of alliances that might
produce other forms of resistance and develop a
sense of agency that does not derive its legitimacy
from power and violence.

Given that analytical work on masculinity as a
gender category has developed relatively recently in
comparison to the long history of feminism, we
must exercise caution as we engage in the deconstruction of the masculine gender. We cannot
approach this work with foolish optimism, since we
have to keep in mind that the deconstruction of
hegemonic masculinity might lead us to construct
new masculinities that end up being neither new
nor desirable, as was the case with groups in the
United States in the 1980s that ended up reaffirming
traditional masculinity. Another example is found
with the endriago subjects we have analyzed in this
book, who are simultaneously subjects of rebellion
and servitude, representing one of the *contradictory
multitudes* that Paolo Virno described. Virno defines
these multitudes as "a way of being that is open to
contradictory developments: rebellion or servitude,

a non-state public sphere or a mass base for authoritarian governments, abolition of subservient labor or *limitless flexibility*. The multitude is ... an inevitable point of departure, albeit ambivalent in nature" (Virno, 2003, 19).

In the face of these *contradictory multitudes*, Virno warns us that if we are to avoid reifying them, we should take care not to interpret them through the (masculinist and hierarchical) tropes of *revolutionary subjects par excellence*. If we want to encourage the deconstruction of hegemonic masculinity, we should not structure our thinking in this way. We also need to be conscious that inciting change and the creation of new masculinities is a double-edged sword: the outcome can be unpredictable and dystopic, if we do not cultivate a radical self-criticality, understanding "radical" in its etymological sense as a return to the root of things.

Thus, it is crucial that the deconstruction of masculinity and the creation of a plurality of masculinities go hand in hand with gender-based perspectives and transfeminism. By transfeminism, we mean not only a social movement made up of women, but also as an epistemological category for the conception and creation of new, non-dystopian—feminine and masculine—identities. It is essential to avoid grounding ourselves in dichotomous and hierarchical understandings of gender for the construction of new alliances between subjects. Since what we know about the multiplicity of genders is actually very little, we regularly lapse solipsistically into constructing the identity of the Other using clichés and stereotypes or projections of our own identity. Clearly, this will not help us to create anything new, since it does not proceed from categories devised outside of the dichotomies that attempt to forge identities, instead of formulating positions. A man is not a woman, and vice versa, but neither is he a man. Or a woman is not a woman either outside of the discourse that upholds her as such.

We think it is incredibly important, as a strategy and as men deconstruct and reinvent masculinity, that they create spaces for themselves outside of the limits set by the heteropatriarchy and violence as a tool for male self-affirmation. In this respect, Itziar Ziga urges us to subvert the patriarchal order:

> I am inspired by the activist Javier Saéz when he says that bears and leather queens embody a betrayal of machismo. These bearded gentlemen with their stocky builds and hairy chests look like real men and not *fucking faggots*; their fate was to subjugate women and they prefer to stick rock-hard fists into each other's forbidden orifices… It is very troubling for the heteropatriarchy to find out that their plumber—with his work overalls, hairy chest, beard and testosterone-fueled image—might actually be gay. That's where the betrayal

Javier mentions is situated. Men who use the identity markers of machismo to undermine them, to embody the most abhorrent specter in the never-ending list of male fears: at base, to be a faggot. … There is no identity more isolated and besieged than the macho male. Not for one instant would I want to be in the skin of those men who have to assault and humiliate faggots and women constantly just to remind themselves that there is nothing feminine (i.e. inferior) lurking inside of them. Just to confirm that they uphold a hegemonic system that, deep down, they know is a sham. *Because in the long run the burden of performing in the theater of the masculine becomes unbearable.* (Ziga, 2009, 119–120)

We need to remove the stigma that is attached to the behaviors of lesbian, gay, bisexual, transsexual, and intersex people, and analyze the achievements of the queer[7] movement in regard to the reinvention of subjectivity. This is because the movement is not based on identities per se, but rather it posits itself as a practical positioning in the face of power. The practices of the queer movement have mounted an effective, public resistance that is not based on sexual preferences or a specific essence; in fact, the movement's primary critique has been to disavow essence, seeing it as reactionary and oppressive. As Paul B. Preciado has written,

The queer movement is post-homosexual and post-gay. It is no longer defined in accordance with medical ideas of homosexuality, but neither does it acquiesce to the reduction of gay identity to a viable lifestyle within neoliberal, consumerist society. It is therefore a post-identitarian movement: queer is not just another identity in multicultural folklore, but rather a critical position mindful of processes of exclusion and marginalization generated by all identitarian fictions. The queer movement is not a movement of homosexuals and gays, but rather of gender and sexual dissidents who resist the norms imposed by dominant, heterosexual society. It is also mindful of internal processes of normalization and exclusion within gay culture: marginalization of dykes, of transexuals and transgender people, of immigrants, of workers and sex workers ... being a *faggot* is not enough to be *queer*: you need to subject your identity to critique. (Preciado, 2009b, 16)

In other words, this resistance shows us that "countless processes of minoritization traverse society" (Guattari & Rolnik, 2008, 103), but also that these processes are traversed by society, making biopolitics reversible. In the face of physical violence and recalcitrant oppression used by the conservative hegemonic system—currently in the form of gore capitalism—disobedience and ingovernability can arrive in channels disregarded by social legitimacy and reviled by patriarchal machismo.

The queer movement does not appeal to normalization as a synonym for legitimacy; in the face of the monopoly of legitimate and illegitimate violence, there are resistance fronts that can mix their agency with a vision of anti-capitalist, playful-critical activism, without this having to be understood in an abstract or superficial way. This resistance work implies a certain level of self-criticism and a reflection on the role of queer resistance in the face of consumerism:

> Consumption also conditions our bodies, determining their forms, traversing our identities and demanding that our affects be registered with an approved framework. We do not want to live in a commercialized ghetto where you only exist as a weekend gay-trans-lesbian, where relationships are commodified and you only have access to this supposed "existence" through spending money. We do not want to consume just to end up being consumed by the same machinery that oppresses us. (Manifesto, 2009)

The queer model then represents: a deconstruction of sexist, heteropatriarchal thought, since it "speaks to a critical project that is an heir to feminist and anti-colonial traditions" (Preciado, 2009b, 17). Of course, this is not the panacea, but it does provide some reference points for other possibilities for interpretation and construction/deconstruction of subjectivity outside of the rigid columns of genders with their demands and investments. We also know that one of the recurring critiques of queerness is that it is thought to be inapplicable in other contexts outside of the United States, where it was called queer theory. Nonetheless, we need to point out that the practices that queer theory attempts to encompass are not exclusive to the U.S., but rather are oppositional resistance practices that have evolved simultaneously worldwide. These practices form forces of non-predatory resistance under a wide variety of diverse names—or at times not even named at all.

Non-normative representations of queer subjects are seen and judged pejoratively because "their mere presence blurs the boundaries between categories previously divided by rationality and decorum" (Preciado, 2009b, 17) and thus they are reviled. When this ceases to be the case, we will be able to realize that the characteristics supposedly "exclusive" to each of the sexes do not exist as such, but rather they can be playfully combined in ways that permit new forms of discourse and a new way to take action.

Thus, masculinities cannot be understood as new if they are disconnected from transfeminism, the queer movement, and minority becoming, or if they are not able to disconnect themselves from obedience and investment in masculinity as understood by power and hegemonic discourse. In other words, the reconfiguration of these new masculinities as a way of forging non-dystopian subjectivities must be linked with resistance, but without linking them to the implementation of power in vertical and heteropatriarchal ways. This leads us to the problem of rethinking the concept and exercise of politics under these conditions of becoming-queer. Politics must be understood through the attributes of queer multitudes:

> Our problem is no longer how to govern populations that have become free, but rather how—across all of our shared spaces—to construct a discourse that takes into account our commonly shared reality, a discourse that would allow us not to be prisoners of voracious and predatory elites over and over again, those same elites who condemn us to persevere submissively as a kind of lesser evil. As the elder scholar Spinoza said, the enemy of the political body is inside of it, and its danger is in the particulars that, as particulars, take hold of power. One of the first requirements of any new politics will have to be taking care of and protecting the collective and shared nature of power itself, understood now not as the power to

govern others, but rather as relations of mutual dependence in a shared space. (Galcerán, 2009, 198–9)

Any reassessment of masculinities that takes into account both becoming-woman and becoming-queer confronts the challenge of building ourselves on a foundation distinct from the well-known dichotomies that tie us to immobilizing and destructive discourses that continue along the same well-traveled paths and arrive at the same conclusions. Faced with these dichotomies, in this book we have posited strategies for deconstructing these discourses. Gender disobedience and the recovery of *backdoor* methodologies and practices have been used by the queer movement to deconstruct this discursive dyad in order to forge other possible, plausible forms of resistance that lead to the enactment of *living revolutions*. In other words, "it will be about setting up networks, putting forward strategies for cultural translation, sharing processes of collective experimentation, rather than labeling delocalizable revolutionary models" (Preciado, 2009a). These revolutions will converge around the creation of a critique within discourse, and strategic, physical resistance that avoids joining the ranks of the victimizers and/or the ranks of the victims of the violence enacted worldwide by the endriago subjects of gore capitalism.

Conclusions

We began this book with the goal of establishing a discourse with sufficient explanatory power to help us translate the *fronterizo* reality of gore capitalism and its creation of an epistemic displacement grounded in violence, drug trafficking, and necropower. In addition, this discourse has attempted to elucidate some of the dystopias of globalization—and their imposition as physical violence on bodies—which are normally unseen in anti-globalization discourses of resistance. We also posited that this discursive approach would be centered on a transfeminist and geopolitically-located perspective. At the same time, we attempted to answer two questions: 1) What kind of subjects and practices are created in this evolution of extreme neoliberalism that we name here as gore capitalism? and 2) How can feminisms—understood both as epistemological tools, as well as theories and social movements—redirect and propose other models for the creation of subjects that are not allied with gore dystopias or with neoliberal hyperconsumerism?

First, within our project we have tasked ourselves with creating discursive taxonomies in situ in order to clearly examine the reality of gore capitalism. The following terms have been important for laying out the discursive map of the phenomenon we sought to analyze: *endriago subject*, *narco-nation*, *nation-market*, *necropower*, *necroempowerment*, *necropractices*, *thanatophilia*, *criminal class*, *gore proletariat*, *piracy of crime*, *gore consumption*, *decorative violence*, and *biomarket*. We are aware that this set of discursive terms is not exhaustive nor does it fully describe the phenomenon. However, our primary interest is to foment the continued expansion of the list of terms used to discuss and elucidate gore capitalism. If that occurs, there will be increased opportunities for consideration, explanation, and articulation of this phenomenon, building a discursive corpus that allows for increased understanding of it; in this regard, this work has largely accomplished its object of examining it and creating a discourse around it.

With respect to the first questions we posited at the beginning of this work, we have concluded that the subjectivities operating within and characteristic of gore capitalism are endriago subjects, who have created a kind of new international class that we have called *the criminal class*. These endriago subjectivities use crime and overt violence as tools for meeting the demands of hyperconsumerist society and its processes of capitalist subjectification. What they have found is a form of socialization through consumption and a practical questioning of the legitimacy of the State and the exercise of violence and hypervigilance as a form of control characteristic of state biopolitics.

Using the example of the war between drug cartels and the Mexican state, we analyzed the battle waged by endriagos against the State (and vice versa) to acquire absolute control of the exercise of violence as a tool for enrichment and necroempowerment. On one hand, this struggle demonstrates that the violence linked to drug-trafficking reinterprets the class struggle and leads to a kind of postcolonialism *in extremis*, recolonized by hyperconsumption and frustration. On the other hand, the fact that endriago subjects wrest power from the State, taking over some of its functions with bloodshed, is factual proof of a real possibility for disobedience and ingovernability within systems of lawful control. Nonetheless, the consequences of these actions end up being unacceptable for those populations who become objects of that violence. Concurrently, we have analyzed how these real, predatory, and necroempowering forms of disobedience dissent from the rules made at the center of power, while always already reaffirming an economic and gendered obedience that is unquestionable for these same subjects. These subjects open a space for belonging and dissidence within the capitalist system, and yet they also preserve masculinist hierarchies; in the end, there is little possibility of interpreting the actions of endriago subjects as effective resistance actions, since their ingovernability is tied to a program that has been previously defined by a violent, hegemonic, capitalist, masculinist framework. Nonetheless, we do not ignore the fact that the resistance of endriago subjects—despite being part of a *contradictory multitude*—does make it discursively possible to think about the need for an effective, non-dystopian dissidence necessarily aligned with questions of gender disobedience and transfeminism. It must create shared alternatives that spur the active participation of civil society.

In response to the second question, we have reflected on the connections between (trans)feminism and gore capitalism. The links between them result from both having arisen within the context of globalization and its demands; both are forms of dissidence and struggle, though clearly with distinct intentions. In this sense, transfeminism is posited as a possible way to chart a different course and to envision other kinds of non-dystopian resistance in the face of gore capitalism's endriago subjectivities. Transfeminism shows us that this resistance must emerge out of alliances that are not grounded in nationalist, identitarian or essentialist precepts, but rather they should debunk these ideas, as *they are profoundly reactionary even when used by progressive movements*. This would open the way for participation, resistance, and agency for those we have called here the *becoming-queer*, thus placing performative actions within both discourse and resistance. These actions have already found a place in social practices by overturning practices of symbolic violence enacted through language, as well as through the occupation/manifestation/visibilization of dissidence in public as well as in private and academic spaces.

Faced with a model of Western thought that understands endriago subjects as products of the unchecked geopolitical dynamics of the First World, we call for the inclusion in discourse of the aforementioned terms that help to explain gore capitalism. While it is true that the phenomenon is more visible in border and Third World spaces, this does not make these terms irrelevant to attempts to explain future variations of gore capitalism that are already emerging—though hardly visible—in the First World. It is an undeniable fact that gore capitalism's endriago subjects have an intimate relationship with the ways that masculinity is articulated and reaffirmed in many cultures. We are aware that the way masculinity is performed is relational, contextual and culturally contingent. Nonetheless, there are some characteristics of hegemonic masculinity that show up again and again; for example, one of these is the show of virility through violence, embodied quite literally by endriago subjects (Bourdieu, 2000, 67–71).

We are not trying to paint gore capitalism as a homogenous phenomenon across cultures, nor do we claim that its variations can be read using everywhere the same categories we propose. However, we suggest that our research can function as a guide map for understanding the realities of gore capitalism. Gore phenomena in the Third World should not be read (by Western thought) as a fragmentation that shows failures in the application of the system, since this hierarchical and (neo)colonialist way of interpreting Third World realities prevents us from thinking about these *fragmentations* from other perspectives. It prevents us from foreseeing how Third World "failures" are not just the result of an incomplete and ill-applied project—modernity and the State, as Gayatri Spivak reminds us, are the property of Europe—but also a premonition, an omen of the fate awaiting the First World in the future. The global logic of capitalism has meant gore has appeared in the Third World at an accelerated rate and in an intensely visible way.

We have pointed out the relationships between the economy of the First World, international legal financial markets, Third World economies and illegal markets tied to trafficking of drugs, weapons and people. Our analysis has focused on drug-trafficking in Mexico and the official and extra-official discourses surrounding it, as it is the arena in which a large number of endriago subjects have developed along with the power dynamics of the gore economy and global capitalism.

Another key point throughout this investigation of gore capitalism is the importance of thinking through the relationship between physical, symbolic, media, and bodily violence. One of the fundamental characteristics of gore capitalism is brutal violence. Throughout this book, we have called for more reflection about the phenomenon of gore capitalism's links to physical violence suffered by spectralized bodies and in the lives of those of us inhabiting the ominous gaps, the spaces considered *outside of* and therefore unworthy of attention. We have attempted to make these lives more visible and to transform them into lives that do not just exist but are worthy of being lived. Nevertheless, we are not calling for the complete elimination of the capitalist system, since it would be delusional to suggest the complete elimination of a system that is so interwoven with our lives and so revered by society. We are also aware that the process of elaborating a critique of gore capitalism will not be "neat [in terms of essentialist purity] nor pretty, nor quick" (Moraga & Anzaldúa, 1983, 191). We do not expect it to be so, but rather we hope that by making the violence visible, we might create a critical consciousness and resistance that could lead to active engagement and the joint creation of responsible intersubjective agreements, endowed with agency. With this, we hope to question the infallibility of the systems of thought used both by conservative neoliberalism as well as by a heteronormative left that has not been able to shake off the foundational dichotomies of Western thought, which are unhelpful in engaging contemporary reality.

The force of *corporeal politics* is founded on the fact that our bodies are repositories of all actions; they are relational and can be understood as integral and active parts of events, as vehicles and linkages of socialization, the first and last enclaves that all of us share. This should not lead us into essentialist, victimist, soft or apolitical positions, but on the contrary into politically committed and (trans)feminist positions that put bodies (in their multiple gradations) into the very center of discussions of gore capitalism, seeing as how they are the most intimate and mutually shared reference point able to link all of us together. As Judith Butler has written,

This means that each of us is constructed politically in part by virtue of the social vulnerability of our bodies—as a site of desire and physical vulnerability, as a site of a publicity at once assertive and exposed. Loss and vulnerability seem to follow from our being socially constituted bodies, attached to others, at risk of losing those attachments, exposed to others, at risk of violence by that exposure. (Butler, 2006, 20)

If we *build politically by virtue of the vulnerability of our bodies*, then we have to recognize the vulnerability of the body as something indisputable. Violence then becomes an extreme act of an other against me, the demonstration of the worst order possible, "a way in which we are given over, without control, to the will of another, a way in which life itself can be expunged by the willful action of another" (Butler, 2006, 29). The violence of gore capitalism is something that cuts across all sectors and surpasses all of us, including the endriago subjects who wield it as their weapon, since "vulnerability ... becomes highly exacerbated under certain social and political conditions, especially those in which violence is a way of life and the means to secure self-defense are limited" (Butler, 2006, 29).

We must remember that the distribution of vulnerability and violence obeys geopolitical structures, but relative geopolitical distance or proximity does not exempt us from responsibility for the physical lives of others. We should work against the feeling that First World security might prevent us from recognizing the radically unequal forms of global distribution of physical vulnerability, since "to foreclose that vulnerability, to banish it, to make ourselves secure at the expense of every other human consideration is to eradicate one of the most important resources from which we must take our bearings and find our way" (Butler, 2006, 30).

Thinking through our bodies is a way to question the unidirectionality of political and economic norms, on a search for other channels. Thus, we must think of pain as a political resource that must not confine us to inaction, but rather might lead us to the development of a reflexive process resulting in an identification with suffering itself, the weaving of intersubjective networks capable of demanding the restructuring of what we understand as the economy, and confronting the economy's dystopian consequences that position our bodies as targets.

In order to change this order of things, it's crucial to cease behaviors that ally us with the cult of violence. Thus, we have to avoid romanticizing violence and bestowing it with an aura of glamor, or on the flipside turning it into an inconsequential issue. We must be clear that the media contributes to venerating violence through spectacularization and endless coverage, while simultaneously neglecting to report on its real consequences. No more admiration for super-specialized violence and no more collectively idolizing hired killers, psychopaths, tyrannical rulers, or mafiosos who get rich by destroying bodies. No more deification of this new necrophallogocentric order.

When we speak of bodies as sites of union, we do not posit a normalization or normativization of bodies, but rather the physical and material structure of living things. When we speak of the body, we are referring to the importance of "claim[ing] that our bodies are in a sense *our own* and that we are entitled to claim rights of autonomy over our bodies" (Butler, 2006, 25). Only if we are able to think through the pain produced by violence in other bodies will we be able to reactivate our relationship with them on a real level. Only if we refuse to legitimate that violence and instead think about the lives of those bodies as worthy of preservation will we be able to think of death as a fundamentally dystopian means of empowerment.

Thus, it is crucial to speak of the body, of the violence enacted upon it and suffered within it. The living flesh that is wounded is not a melodramatic metaphor,[1] because it is not a metaphor at all. The importance of a dead body cannot be reduced to an image that lasts two seconds during an afternoon of channel-surfing on television. Flesh and its wounds are real; they cause physical pain to those who suffer the wounds. We also know that positing the body as a foundational concept can be stigmatized as *body reductionism*, but "in contrast, in searching for associative concepts (such as those of 'person,' 'self,' and 'individual') there is an equal danger of reconstituting the liberal eighteenth-century ideal of the 'individual' endowed with 'moral autonomy' as the basis for political theory and political action" (Harvey, 2003, 119).

We urgently need to extricate the body from media discourses that spectralize it, so that we might depict it in all of its potency and importance. If we are able to re-ontologize the body, we will be able to re-semanticize the power of death in the gore capitalist and patriarchal framework. This re-semanticization of the body and its pain will emerge from language, critique, and performative practices that are developed in public space and through *queer multitudes*. We have to return to conceding articulatory power to bodily realities and violence. We have to be able to construct meaning around the death of any person. To make sure that the death and the pain of an Other cause a shudder in all of our bodies. To dismantle the illusion created by news media that artificially naturalizes the exercise of violence, rendering it invisible through the protective distance of the screen, which tells us that extreme non-consensual pain only happens to the bodies of Others.[2]

Re-semanticization of the body cannot be conceived of without deconstruction and criticism of hegemonic masculinity—articulated in the first person. The force of reformulating totalizing masculinity into plural and localized masculinities is grounded in the fact that, in practice, these new masculinities already exist and resist hegemonic masculinity. This force is clearly linked to another force: the deconstruction of patriarchal phallogocentrism that is directly allied with capitalism and the exercise of violence. Violence here becomes first a resource for masculine socialization, and second a crucial tool for obtaining legitimacy through compliance with one of the most important demands of masculinity: access to power through economic enrichment and the superiority that this bestows within the hierarchy of patriarchal and capitalist value. By focusing on new kinds of masculinities, we can re-think the role of endriago subjects.

In addition to paying attention to the resistance practices forged by queer movements to question gender categories, the masculine gender must incorporate other social skills into its practices from an early age, specifically skills which are not directly linked with the exercise of violence as a validation of virility. It is crucial that these skills include an ability to confront one's own suffering in order to develop the capacity to show empathy for the suffering of others. As we map out alternatives for the construction of new masculinities, we must de-link the masculine subject from the concept of *sole economic provider*, given the fact that this demand is not compatible with current economic conditions in light of precarious access to jobs. The inability to fulfill this demand made on men leads to frustration that is often translated into aggressiveness. If we are to end the gender hierarchies that place masculinity in the dominant position, one crucial social task is the development and implementation of a non-sexist education available to all from an early age.

Throughout this book, we have sought a means to explain contemporary conditions and their ties to the inescapable exercise of violence. We have attempted to not mistakenly confuse our argument with either moral absolution or judgment of the violence, because we do not want to be solely circumscribed by moral values; rather our aim has been to re-think the central role of the violence in the evolution of capitalism and its culmination in gore.

We have attempted to present our research work in concert with a transfeminist analysis that might allow us to think beyond the limits of our current options. In other words, in each specific, oppressive context, we have to create theoretical tools and practices that might help us to develop our strategies. When there are no other options to choose from, we must be capable of transforming the sole option not into a withdrawal or death but rather into a condition of resignification. To conclude then, at a time when gore capitalism presents itself globally as the sole option available, we must work so that instead of killing us, it might resignify us and lead us to re-think our very selves.

Finally, gore capitalism is a product of globalization that demonstrates the system's dystopias, but it also demonstrates that "contemporary social subjects are endless. The dimension of the social and ethical I is the center of the disorder" (Villaplana, 2008, 63). In other words, the fissures of the system expose possible means of escape from it, particularly for those subjects who ground their existence in the reinvention of agency through critique, a refusal to adapt, and general disobedience. These subjects trace out paths of defiance that allow them to live in struggle through effective, micropolitical resistance.

El Mero Inicio / The Very Beginning

[Beginning: Date: 12th Century. 1: the point of something begins: START. 2: the first part. 3: ORIGIN, SOURCE. 4: a rudimentary stage or early period—usually used in plural.]

Do you know the History of Mexico?

Well, never mind. There's not much to know.

It's all dust and blood.

—Alan Moore. *Miracleman*

It's 6pm on Boulevard Insurgentes. The cars rush along at prodigious speeds; rush hour in Tijuana is frenzied. I moved away several years ago, and every time I come back the city is an onslaught. I'm driving a gold SUV, and my pre-teen sister is sitting in the passenger seat beside me. Even before I left, Tijuana was always breathtakingly psychopathic. Today though, I discover, right in front of me, a new way of classifying the city. At first I don't realize it, at first I only feel shock, a catatonic daze, the *urge to*, followed by aphasia and impotence. At first, I only have a glazed look in my eyes, a knot in my throat, an urge to scream, to run away, but I can't. I am driving along the boulevard, I see the clock and without knowing why, the specific time embeds itself in my eyes like a bayonet. Perhaps a premonition, maybe the air charged with the leftover bits of gunpowder, dirt, and coke. I chat with my sister, jumping quickly from family traumas to small talk and back again. Just ahead of our car, there is a black pick-up—the latest model, no license plates—and I watch it indifferently. The bed of the truck is piled up with black bags, filled with what I assume is trash.

Between the small talk and my own indifference, the pick-up drops into a dip in the road and one of the bags falls out and tears open just ahead of my moving car. The contents fall out in front of our SUV. The contents are burned into my retinas. I still see the contents some nights falling in slow motion, over and over again. Just ahead of my car, the dismembered torso of a man falls on the ground. A torso that still has its head attached. A young man with dark hair and large eyes, half of a man. I swerve around the body, trying to stop the car, but suddenly I hear the sound of horns honking and I remember I'm driving on an expressway where it's impossible to stop without causing a multiple car pileup. I try to pull myself together. I can't.

I'm gripping the steering wheel with all my strength, my hands trembling. I keep quiet. I don't dare look at my sister. Three minutes later, I can finally glance at her. I look at my sister's face, her long neck and profile. I don't dare look at her whole body. I can't after driving past half of a dead man in the middle of the highway. I try to convince myself that it's not true, that I'm hallucinating, that this time the city has gotten under my skin.

She seems to realize just how terrified I am, and she turns her head to look at me. I ask her in a kind of guttural bark, "What was that?" She puts her hand on my shoulder, as she looks me in the eyes and says, "That was the torso of man who'd been cut into pieces, Sayak. This is Tijuana."

There is no astonishment in her eyes. I can't even find a trace of fear in her voice. There's none of that, just her steady eyes and her voice saying words that I'd hoped wouldn't confirm what I just saw. I want to pull myself together, but I can't. Then, the shock and the catatonic daze, the *urge to*, followed by aphasia and impotence. We arrive home, and I can't shake off the trepidation that every human being should feel upon seeing the corpse of another. That dead man shook me out of my spectralized and comfortable idea of death, ripped me out of the mediatized logic that tells us that bad things always happen to Others. The body makes me realize that I am the Others, without any inkling of humanism, coolness, or dilletantish solidarity. In other words, that dead man reconfirms for me that I am irrevocably marked by gender, race, class, and the geopolitical distribution of vulnerability. That dead man tells me that I am also responsible for his dismemberment, that my passivity as a citizen is crystallized in impunity. That dead man and my sister's emotionless face tell me that I have to do something with this, because if I don't, it'll do something with me.

That is the very beginning.

Notes

Warning / Advertencia

1. The term g-local refers in economic terms to the fact that the economy and the production of meaning are conceived of globally and implemented locally.

2. "Terms like 'third' and 'first' world are very problematical as they suggest over-simplified similarities between and amongst countries labelled 'third' or 'first' world, as well as implicitly reinforcing existing economic, cultural and ideological hierarchies" (Chandra Talpade Mohanty. "Under Western Eyes: Feminist Scholarship and Colonial Discourses"). Thus we will use both terms in a critical way. Above all, we will use the term Third World to refer to a world that, given its conditions, maps out its own distinct strategies for empowerment.

3. Butler (2006), p. 69.

Introduction

1. We use necroempowerment to designate the processes that transform contexts and/or situations of vulnerability and/or subalternity into possibilities for action and self-empowerment, and that reconfigure these situations through dystopian practices and a perverse self-affirmation achieved through violent means.

2. Here we understand capital in the quotidian sense of access to wealth, and to the accumulation of money that gives subjects access to a certain social mobility, to a change in status, to a legitimacy bestowed by their capacity to join the ranks of the market's hyperconsumers.

3. According to the Oxford English Dictionary, the term "dystopia" was coined in the late nineteenth century by John Stuart Mill as an antonym for Thomas More's utopia; the term sought to designate a negative utopia, in which reality would proceed along tracks antithetical to those of an ideal society (http://www.oed.com).

4. It is worth mentioning that the data used to estimate the size of the criminal economy is approximate due to how difficult it is to verify. Both Curbet (2007) and Resa in "El crimen organizado en el mundo: mito y realidad" [Organized Crime in the World: Myth and Reality] (2004) are in agreement about this difficulty.

5. The gradual resurgence and subsequent boom in piracy at the Somali port of Eyl over the last two decades (and its intensification since 2008) accounts for Pratt's 2002 statement. This type of activity has become extremely profitable, giving rise to noteworthy paradoxes like the fact that crime has become desirable as a profession: "The criminals' weaponry is now so sophisticated, their earnings so impressive and their quality of life so appealingly high that the young men in this coastal settlement of Eyl, in deeply impoverished Somalia, want to be pirates" (Aznárez, 2008, 6). This is a complete break with Western logics, yet it is perfectly understandable that this has happened, since as some of the pirates explain, "What forced us to become pirates was that foreign fleets stole our fisheries. Now we collect it back through the ransoms. Hunger made us pirates" (Ibid). Such networks are difficult to dismantle since even though, "pirate seafaring is limited, the majority of the population participates indirectly in the business" (Ibid). It is widely known that crime and the underground economy derive from necessity, bad governance and official corruption; this makes it clear that neither the piracy issue in Somalia nor the problem of the Mexican cartels can be dealt with effectively until these countries are guaranteed a sustainable economic stability over the mid- and long-term.

6. Terms used to refer to human traffickers in Latin America, especially in Mexico.

A Clarification About Gore: Becoming-Snuff

1. Splatter or gore films are a type of horror movie focused on blood-shed and graphic violence. Through the use of special effects and an excessive amount of artificial blood, these films attempt to display the vulnerability of the human body and to dramatize its mutilation. Snuff films, on the other hand, are recordings of real murders (without the assistance of special effects or any other kind of trick). Their end goal is to record these atrocities with AV equipment and then later to distribute them commercially as entertainment.

2. We believe it is accurate to combine the term capitalism with these two film genres, since in our mass media era, film (still) constructs a large portion of the cultural imaginary, while simultaneously the U.S. film industry remains one of the most powerful representatives of contemporary capitalism.

1. The Breakdown of the State as a Political Formation

1. Cfr Agamben (2003). Cfr. Agamben. In this text, Agamben investigates the reinforcement of structures of power that governments employ in supposed periods of crisis. Agamben refers to the extension of power in these periods as states of exception, in which the diminishment, replacement or rejection of citizenship and individual rights is justified by the extension of power itself. Or, as Agamben explains it: "In every case, the state of exception marks a threshold at which logic and praxis blur with each other and a pure violence without logos claims to realize an enunciation without any real reference." Thus Agamben's state of exception is a situation in which the suspension of laws in a state of emergency or crisis becomes a prolonged state of being.

2. This process is comparable to the one that took place in Mexico in the 1970s, in which B-movies and the popular musical genre of the corrido began to establish a new identity related to drug culture—an identity which has contributed to the legitimation and popularization of criminal identity as desirable.

3. Globalization proposes that we are all equal before the display-windows of consumption and the portals of cyberspace. This equality merely means that we all share the same possibilities of

desiring the same things. But even this system of abstract leveling is undermined by the insistent difference between the desire to have and the ability to have.

4. A recurring question for nationalism is the issue of language, which the majority of nationalist discourses view as a central axis of unity and as a rationale. But this fact must be contrasted with the growing popularity and "need" to learn the English language: the language of business, money, and economic exchange; this popularity is no coincidence but is in fact a point of convergence between the nation-market and various nationalisms. The expansion of a single language is dangerous not only because of its diffusion of the economics-driven world-view through various media, but also because it has epistemological effects, foreclosing the very possibility of thinking and expressing certain ideas.

5. Resa, TK. Carlos Resa Nestares is Professor of Applied Economics in the Department of Economic Structure and Development Economics at the Universidad Autónoma de Madrid. Peyote, Inc. was a business founded in 2003 to provide consulting services in matters related to organized crime. The company's area of expertise included multiple sectors of organized crime, but with a special focus on Mexico's illegal drug traffic. Peyote Inc. counts among its clients public institutions, private entities, and international organizations.

6. On this topic, Jaume Curbet has pointed out that "only 1% of the profits from the drug trade remain in the hands of the farmers who engage in the clandestine cultivation of the crops. This means that as little as a 2% increase in worldwide development assistance would be enough to compensate for the deficit of the farmers, if they were inclined to engage in the cultivation of farm products" (Curbet, 2007, 69–70).

7. See the work of the Interdisciplinary Collaborative La Línea, http://feariseffective.blogspot.com.

8. This lack of concern also reflects a gender bias, particularly evident in the scarce interest the government has shown in the feminicidios in Ciudad Juárez.

9. PRI is the acronym for the Institutional Revolutionary Party (Partido Revolucionario Institucional), which held power from 1929 to 2000. PAN is the acronym for the conservative, Christian-Democratic National Action Party (Partido Acción Nacional), which won the presidential elections in 2000 and maintained presidential power until 2012.

10. Capitalism sustains itself on a patriarchal system that foments competition and ceaselessly puts "manliness" (understood as a fundamental element of social legitimation) to the test. See Bourdieu (2000).

11. http://www.materiabiz.com/mbz/entrepreneurship/index.vsp

12. Narco-banners are sheets hung primarily from bridges or places of heavy traffic in Mexican cities, handwritten with messages conveying extreme defiance or ridicule of the legitimate government. These messages are an attempt to recruit civilians and elite soldiers alike to join the company, that is to swell the ranks of the narcos.

2. Capitalism as Cultural Construction

1. Translator's Note: In the original Spanish-language edition of *Capitalismo Gore*, Valencia used Preciado's pre-transition name, which he used at the time of writing of the original book. In this translation into English, Preciado's name has been updated to reflect his subsequent transition.

2. For a deeper analysis of this topic, see Jiménez and Tena (2007).

3. The concept of the feminization of labor carries an implicitly sexist double meaning. In the first place, it renders the work of women throughout history invisible by suggesting that this is the first period in which women have worked, erasing unpaid labor as women's manifest destiny and natural fate. Second, there is a gendered logic to the idea that women's work is continually characterized as flexible, mobile, mutable, badly paid and precarious, while men's work is characterized as secure, stable, well-paid, and reliable. For more on this topic, see Precarias a la Deriva (2004).

4. We understand the concept of artificial naturalization, in the Bourdieusian sense of the term, to refer to practices and concepts as socially-naturalized constructions that de-historicize and introduce a false genealogy based on a temporality that fades over time. This false genealogy creates the idea that certain things have been the same since the very beginning and for that reason they are phenomena or concepts that should be understood as natural (Bourdieu, 2000).

5. Strategies based on other people's deaths as tools for wealth acquisition.

6. We are using this metaphor because we understand an aleph to be "the only place on earth where all places are—seen from every angle, each standing clear, without any confusion or blending" (Borges, 1970).

7. See the talk by Denisse Dresser: https://www.youtube.com/watch?v=CtB4MWq4QxM

8. I am referring here to the boom in alternative churches that venerate death itself in the form of the Santa Muerte figure, elevating death to the level of sainthood. In this way, they have created a fairly unique syncretic faith that mixes Catholic and pagan practices. This syncretism is reflected in the fact that the figure of Santa Muerte is taken up and transformed into a deity that stands in opposition to all the religious beliefs of the Catholic Church. The cult of Santa Muerte has assumed a central place for everyone involved in crime. In Sinaloa, we also find the cult of Malverde, known as the narco saint. The Malverde cult establishes the narco's code of moral justification: law and justice are not the same thing.

9. François Houtart claims that in 2002, Sri Lanka had the highest suicide rate in the world, the majority of them small-scale agricultural workers (see Estévez and Taibo, 2008, 29).

10. As confirmed by Forbes Magazine's inclusion of a Mexican drug trafficker in its 2009 list of the world's richest men.

11. We need to begin by critiquing the received meanings of terms like colonialism, decolonialism, and postcolonialism. We must acknowledge that until our minds have achieved a critical distance

and separation from colonialism, we cannot speak of decolonization or postcolonization. In Mexico, specifically, what we see is a
certain continuation of colonial thinking in everyday life that
becomes visible through (often internalized) microphobias and
explicit racism against indigenous people. We have to recognize
and accept that we are still mentally colonized, and moreover that
both Mexican independence and the revolution were illusions of a
change that was never actually instituted and has not taken place.
We continue to allow foreign discourses to dominate, as we uncriti-
cally accept them as our own. We have been sold the myth of our
decolonization, and we have bought wholesale the notion that we
are a developing nation with a hunger for modernity. We have
been fed a diet of rhetoric and stereotypes. In all spheres (from
academia to the realm of daily life), we are still happy to embody
European identities that have little to do with our own needs, our
economic practices, and our geopolitical subjectivities.

12. In this regard, see Mignolo (2003a).

13. This Third World is not exclusively located in territories
understood as faraway countries with depressed economies; rather,
there are pockets of Third World conditions in the nerve centers of
First World capitalism.

14. Zubero, Imanol (Doctor of Sociology. Member of Gesture
for Peace [Gesto por la Paz].) This quote is a paraphrase of scene
four from *Macbeth* by William Shakespeare. Quote from
Medem (2003).

15. It is important to state that the endriago subjectivities we are
positing here have no relation to the interpretation the Nazis gave
to the blond beasts. We take Nietzche's concept as referring to
excessive and violent subjectivities.

16. This is another paradox of globalization, since one of its fundamental dictums has to do with the elimination of borders, and
yet, the borders that are opened are those that allow for the flow of
capital, but not for people.

17. *Amadís de Gaula* is a masterpiece of fantastic medieval literature in Spanish and the most famous of the so-called *libros de*

caballería [books of chivalry], which were extremely popular during the sixteenth century on the Iberian peninsula.

18. Amadis of Gaul represents both the knight and the inherited values of Western culture generally. Amadis is the Western subject par excellence, the non-monster, the non-Other, namely the universal, un-fractured subject who later would be defended by the Enlightenment and humanism.

19. By border territories, we are referring to borders in general, but we emphasize the borders in Northern Mexico that are next to the United States and especially Tijuana, Ciudad Juárez, and Tamaulipas. These zones are perfect examples of the aforementioned situation, as they are territories which have been overrun for decades by drug cartels, human-traffickers, prostitution and a variety of repressive State forces. This has created a battlefield, a territory in a perpetual state of siege.

3. The New Mafia

1. See Schumpeter (1942).

2. This practice is interesting on both a material and symbolic level. At the material level, it is a practice that implies a symbiosis between work and death, because the invention of the guillotine can be understood as the beginning of the industrialization of death itself. On a symbolic level, decapitation enacts an erasure of the identity of the victim's bodily identity. For the aggressor, removing the victim's head is a demonstration of the veracity and the effectiveness of the crime, granting the aggressor a kind of legitimacy. What's more, there is a strange proximity between the words decapitation and decapitalization, which functions in some way like this: each decapitation is a decapitalization of the legal economic system and an interrogation of state authority.

3. For further analysis of the figure of the schizo, see Deleuze and Guattari: *Anti-Oedipus: Capitalism and Schizophrenia*, Minneapolis, University of Minnesota Press, 1983.

4. Misha Glenny argues that currently British Columbia is the wellspring of a flourishing industry dedicated to growing and distributing marijuana. See Glenny, 2008, chapter 10.

5. This is the case for methamphetamines, which were developed by Nazi chemists so that their soldiers would be able to withstand cold, hunger, and terror. Their use has become widespread in wealthy countries like the United States where they are consumed by large sectors of the population as a form of leisure or in poor countries like Thailand (where drug trafficking is punished with the death penalty and consumption is also severely punished). In Thailand, methamphetamines are known as *yaba*, and they are used by all of the most marginal sectors of the population, like workers who are forced to endure grueling work days.

6. Diane Coyle is a professor at the University of Manchester, columnist for The Independent and director of a consulting business, Enlightenment Economics.

7. These networks dedicated to piracy of crime have been established not only along the Mexican border but also have been able to grow to staggering levels across Mexico.

4. Necropolitics

1. As David Harvey indicates, the investigation into "the body as the irreducible locus for the determination of all values, meanings, and significations is not new. It was fundamental to many strains of pre-Socratic philosophy and the idea that 'man' or 'the body' is 'the measure of all things' has had a long and interesting history." Further, "the resurrection of interest in the body in contemporary debates [is clear in the work of] feminists and queer theorists [who] have pioneered the way as they have sought to unravel issues of gender and sexuality in theory and political practices" (Harvey, 2000, 97–8).

2. Currently, there is an increasing similarity between Colombia and Mexico with respect to the problem of violence and the necropolitical management of life; however, that is beyond the scope of this work.

3. Within earlier forms of capitalist production, forms of production and consumption were linked with one another in a direct and apparently inextricable way; in the present day, this has changed. We use the term biomarket to refer to this shift.

4. Foucault (1994), p. 729.

5. Derrida (1998), p. 147.

6. An acronym for Avtomat Kalashnikov model 1947, AK-47 is a Soviet assault weapon designed in 1947 by Mikhael Kalashnikov, a Russian soldier during the Second World War. In 1949, the Red Army adopted it as the primary weapon in the infantry, though it was not used on a massive scale until 1954. Today, it is estimated that these weapons are the ones used most by internal guerrilla groups and rebel groups around the world (for example, the FARC in Colombia), criminal networks, and global mafias.

7. To see images of these artifacts, see Philliphe Stack: http://www.starck.com

8. For images of these vehicles, see: http://www.hummer.com

9. The new capitalism is the same savage capitalism but now unmasked and without any attempts to hide its guilt. It is a more cynical and bloody capitalism, a grotesque, bizarre and excessively violent capitalism with no big-budget special effects: a gore capitalism.

10. We are referring to the effect discussed by Mike Davis (2002, 6) and proposed by the Israeli psychoanalyst Yolanda Gampel, who understand the effect of interminable uncanniness as "a sensibility that usurps the lives of those who have witnessed an 'astounding, unbelievable, and unreal reality,' like mass murder. 'They no longer fully believed their own eyes: they had difficulty distinguishing between this unreal reality and their own imagination.'" Gampel cited in Mike Davis, 2002, 6.

11. The primary difference between derealization and fiction is that the former is a tactic of war that aims to identify the Other as an enemy in order to be able to kill them. Fiction is everything that is not real, that is a representation and plays, or doesn't play, with symbolic concepts of the real but does not seek to be faithful to reality. (See the concept of a simulacrum in Baudrillard.)

12. There are clear segregationist and racist valences implied by this ethnic identification. At the beginning of the twentieth century, the Italian community in the United States was highly monitored and

widely condemned. The ethnic origin of the main character can thus be understood as a way to exoticize and legitimate his criminal practices, locating him outside of the bounds of legality, since he is not an Anglo (white) U.S. American in the strictest sense of the term.

13. "Machismo is a discourse of inequality. It consists of discrimination based on the belief that men are superior to women. In practice, machismo is used to refer to acts or words that—usually in an offensive or vulgar way—demonstrate the sexism underlying the social structure … Sexism is defined as the set of methods used by the patriarchy to maintain the subjugated female sex in a position of inferiority, subordination, and exploitation. Sexism impacts all levels of life and human relations" (Varela, 2005, 180).

14. Rupert Murdoch is the owner of the ultraconservative channel Fox News and many other media outlets in the real world.

15. It is worth mentioning that some of the game's players argue that this videogame should not be judged apart from its context. Nevertheless, the newspaper Citizen Tribune reported that this videogame led two teenagers ages 16 and 13—the Williams brothers—to become snipers. The brothers pled guilty to charges of homicide and aggravated assault for a shooting on June 25, 2003, in which one man was killed and a young woman was injured. Aaron Hamel, a 45-year-old nurse, was shot in the head as he was driving along a highway and Kimberley Bede, a 19-year-old in another car, was shot in her stomach. The techniques used by the Willams brothers copied those used in the game, since "the game trains players on how to aim and shoot firearms and inspires them so they can do it more accurately" (www.citizentribune.com).

16. In Mexico, in some marginal sectors of the population, Death is elevated to the level of a saint. This saint has attracted many worshippers. We have already mentioned this relationship between La Santa Muerte and the world of crime in chapters one and two.

17. This is the term applied to the tactic of warfare used to dehumanize the other and to identify them as an enemy, in order to annihilate them.

18. See Vidal Beneyto quoted in Estévez & Taibo (2008) p. 95.

5. At the Brink of El Bordo, I Become Blade

1. Here we are drawing a parallel between the expansionist policies of the United States that justified the conquest of territory as a divine, patriarchal right with the occupation/oppression/destruction of women's bodies and actions as a conquered territory belonging to the patriarchy.

2. Cfr. Connell, Robert W. (1999). Der Gemachte Mann. Konstruktion von Männlichkeiten..Opladen. pp. 95–102.

3. Translator's Note: Throughout this book, *transfeminismo* is translated as transfeminism; despite this, it is critical to note the differences between transfeminism in the anglophone world and *transfeminismo* in Spain and Latin America. In their introduction to the 2016 issue of the Transgender Studies Quarterly on *Trans/Feminisms*, Susan Stryker and Talia Bettcher write about these differences quite eloquently: "In English, *transfeminism* [...] usually connotes a "third wave" feminist sensibility that focuses on the personal empowerment of women and girls, embraced in an expansive way that includes trans women and girls. It is adept at online activism and makes sophisticated use of social media and Internet technologies; it typically promotes sex positivity (such as support for kink and fetish practices, sex-worker rights, and opposition to "slut shaming") and espouses affirming attitudes toward stigmatized body types (such as fat, disabled, racialized, or trans bodies); it often analyzes and interprets pop cultural texts and artifacts and critiques consumption practices, particularly as they relate to feminine beauty culture. In Spanish and Latin American contexts, *transfeminismo* carries many of these connotations as well, but it has also become closely associated with the "postporn" performance art scene, squatter subcultures, antiausterity politics, post-*Indignado* and post-Occupy "leaderless revolt" movements, and support for immigrants, refugees, and the undocumented; in some contexts, it is understood as a substitute for, and successor to, an anglophone queer theory and activism deemed too disembodied, and too linguistically foreign, to be culturally relevant. *Transfeminismo*, rather than imagining itself as the articulation of a new form of postidentitarian sociality (as queer did), is considered a polemical appropriation of, and a refusal of exclusion

from, existing feminist frameworks that remain vitally necessary; the *trans-* prefix not only signals the inclusion of trans* people as political subjects within feminism but also performs the lexical operation of attaching to, dynamizing, and transforming an existing entity, pulling it in new directions, bringing it into new arrangements with other entities."

4. Intersectionality is a tool to analyze advocacy work and the development of policy that takes into account multiple discriminations and helps us understand the way that different kinds of identities influence people's access to rights and opportunities. To delve deeper into this term, see the work of Kimberley W. Crenshaw. To understand how intersectionality leads to the creation of multiple identities that simultaneously embody oppression and privilege, we recommend looking at the writing of Gloria Anzaldúa, Chela Sandoval, Cherríe Moraga and especially the anthology *This Bridge Called My Back: Writings by Radical Women of Color*.

5. Translator's Note: La Eskalera Karakola is a collective of women who founded an independent feminist community center in an occupied building in the Lavapies neighborhood of Madrid in 1996. *Otras inapropiables* [Unappropriatable Others] is an anthology the collective edited and published with writings by U.S. feminists of color in Spanish translation.

6. We would like to emphasize that we are specifically referring to an analysis of masculinity as it is lived in Latin American contexts. Above all, we do not disregard the fact that there already are some forms of masculine confrontation in these spaces, masculinities that do not share nor obey the dictates of capitalist and masculinist power. To the extent possible, they have been able to detach themselves from the dominant identity in a critical way; however, these detachments have not achieved sufficient visibility.

7. Used since the eighteenth century as an insult, the use of the word "queer" shifted at the end of the 1980s in the United States, when "a conglomeration of microgroups decided to appropriate the insult 'queer' to create a space for political action and resistance to normalization" (Preciado, 2009b, 16).

Conclusions

1. We emphasize the fact that bodily harm should not be understood under the rubric of a victimization-obsessed melodrama, since as Nirmal Puwar argues, following the thinking of R. Chow: "Dishonor and sanctification belong to the same symbolic order: idealization" (Mezzadra et al., 2008, 247).

2. We do not want to disregard the fact that there are certain consensual practices of violence like BDSM, which we understand to be practices enacted from a free, horizontal and voluntary position and not as an imitation of the mechanisms of domination and submission inflicted for centuries by the patriarchy. In this regard, see Junyent (2009) cited in Valencia (2009).

Selected Bibliography

Agamben, Giorgio. 2008. *State of Exception*. University of Chicago Press, Chicago.

Amorós Puente, Celia. 2008. *Mujeres e imaginarios de la globalización; reflexiones para una agenda teórica global del feminismo.* Homo Sapiens Ediciones, Argentina.

Amorós Puente, C. & De Miguel, A. 2005. *Historia de la teoría feminista: de la Ilustración a la Globalización*, Editorial Minerva, Madrid.

Anderson, B. S. Zinsser, J. P. 1991. *Historia de las mujeres: una historia propia*, vol. II, Crítica, Barcelona.

Anderson, Perry. 2000. *Los orígenes de la posmodernidad*, Anagrama, Barcelona.

Anzaldúa, Gloria & Keating, AnaLouise. 2002. *This Bridge We Call Home: Radical Visions for Transformations*, Routledge, New York.

Augé, Marc. 2004. *Los no lugares. Espacios del anonimato. Una antropología de la sobremodernidad*, Gedisa, Barcelona.

Austin, John. 1998. Cómo hacer cosas con palabras, Paidós, Barcelona.

Babel, Isaac. 1920. *Diary*, Yale University Press, New Haven.

Bares, Mauricio. 2007. *Posthumano*, Editorial Almadía, Oaxaca, México.

Barthes, Roland. 1990a. *La aventura semiológica*, Paidós, Barcelona.

———. 1990b. *La cámara lúcida. Nota sobre la fotografía*, Paidós, Barcelona.

Bataille, George. 1986. *Erotism: Death and Sensuality*, Trans. Mary Dalwood, City Lights, San Francisco.

——. 1989. *The Tears of Eros*, City Lights Books, San Francisco.

Baudrillard, Jean. 1996. *The Perfect Crime*, Verso, New York.

——. 2000. *Las estrategias fatales*, Anagrama, Barcelona.

——. 2002. *Contraseñas*, Anagrama, Barcelona.

Benjamín, Walter. 1999. *Para una crítica de la violencia y otros ensayos*, Taurus, Madrid.

——. 2001. *Poesía y capitalismo*, Taurus, Madrid.

——2008. *Tesis sobre la Historia y otros fragmentos*, Editorial Ítaca, México.

Berman, Marshall. 1984. *All That Is Solid Melts into Air: The Experience of Modernity*, Verso, New York.

——. 2001. *Adventures in Marxism*, Verso, New York.

Bernárdez, Asunción (ed.) 2001. *Violencia de género y sociedad: una cuestión de poder*, Ayuntamiento de Madrid, Madrid.

Bloch, Ernst. 2004. *El principio de Esperanza*, Trotta, Madrid.

Bourdieu, Pierre. 1979. *La distinction*, Editions du Minuit, París.

——. 1980. *Le sens pratique*, Editions du Minuit, París.

——. 1997. *Méditations pascaliennes*, Editions du Seuil, París.

——. 2001. *Sobre la televisión*. Anagrama, Barcelona.

——. 2002. *Masculine Domination*. Stanford UP, Palo Alto.

Bourdieu, Pierre & Wacquant, Loïc. 1992. *An Invitation to Reflexive Sociology*, University of Chicago Press, Chicago.

Borges, Jorge Luis. 1999. *Manual de zoología fantástica*, fce, México.

——. 1970. *El Aleph*, Trans. by Norman Thomas Di Giovanni. EP Dutton, New York.

Blondel, Maurice. 2005. *El punto de partida de la investigación filosófica*, Ediciones Encuentro, Madrid.

Böttcher, Nikolaus (eds.) 2005. *Los buenos, los malos y los feos: poder y resistencia en América Latina*, Vervuert, Frankfurt am Main.

Braidotti, Rossi. 2005. *Metamorfosis. Hacia una teoría materialista del devenir*. Akal, Madrid.

Brieva, Miguel. 2009. *Dinero. Revista de Poética Financiera e Intercambio Espiritual*, Random House Mondadori, Barcelona.

Buchanan, Ian & Colebrook, Claire (eds.) 2000. *Deleuze and Feminist Theory*, Edinburgh University Press, Edinburgh.

Burman, E. & Parker, I. (eds.) 1993. *Discourse Analytic Research*, Routledge, London.

Butler, Judith. 2001. *El género en disputa*, Paidós, México.

——. 2004a. *Lenguaje, poder e identidad*, Síntesis, Madrid.

——. 2004b. *Undoing Gender*, Routledge, Nueva York-Londres.

——. 2006. *Precarious Life: The Powers of Mourning and Violence*, Verso, New York.

Cahn, Susan. 1994. *Coming On Strong; Gender and Sexuality in Twentieth-Century Women's Sport*, Harvard University Press, Cambridge.

Carrasco, Cristina. (ed.) 2003. *Mujeres y economía. Nuevas perspectivas para viejos y nuevos problemas*, Icaria, Barcelona.

Castro-Gómez, Santiago 2005. *La hybris del punto cero. Ciencia, raza e ilustración en la Nueva Granada (1750–1816)*, Editorial Pontificia de la Universidad Javeriana, Bogotá.

Chakrovorty Spivak, Gayatri. 1999. *A Critique of Postcolonial Reason. Toward a History of the Vanishing Present*, Harvard University Press, Cambridge, Mass.

Cixous, Hélène. 1995. *La risa de la medusa. Ensayos sobre la escritura, Anthropos*, Madrid.

——. 2004. *Deseo de escritura*, Reverso, Barcelona.

Claramonte, Jordi. 2009. *Lo que puede un cuerpo*, Infraleves, cendeac, Murcia.

Coyle, Diane. 2004. *Sex, Drugs & Economics*, Texere, New York.

Curbet, Jaume. 2007. *Conflictos globales, violencias locales*, flacso, Quito, Ecuador.

Davis, Mike. 2002. *Dead Cities and Other Tales*. New Press, New York.

De Lauretis, Teresa. 2000. *Diferencias*, Horas y HORAS, Madrid.

Del Lagrace Volcano & Dahl Ulrika. 2008. *Femmes of Power. Exploding Queer Femininities*, Serpent's Tail, London.

Deleuze Gilles & Guattari Félix. 1985. *El Anti-Edipo. Capitalismo y esquizofrenia*, Paidós, Barcelona.

Deleuze Gilles. 1989. *El pliegue. Leibniz y el Barroco*, Paidós, Barcelona.

Derrida, Jacques. 1998. *Ecografías de la Televisión*, Eudeba, Buenos Aires.

Despentes, Virginie. 2010. *King Kong Theory*, Feminist Press, New York.

De los Ríos, I., Castro, F., Castro, I., Fresán, R. & Lafuente, F. 2009. *Los Sopranos Forever. Antimanual de una serie de culto*, Errata Naturae, Madrid.

Eco, Humberto. 1983. *Cómo se hace una tesis. Técnicas y procedimientos de investigación, estudio y escritura*, Gedisa, Madrid.

——. 2000. *Tratado de Semiótica General*, Lumen, Barcelona.

Escohotado, Antonio. 1999. *Historia general de las drogas*, Espasa Calpe, Mexico.

Estévez, Carlos & Taibo Carlos (eds.). 2008. *Voces contra la globalización*, Crítica, Barcelona.

Finkielkraut, Alan. 1995. *The Defeat of the Mind*, Columbia University Press, New York.

Foucault, Michel. 1977. *Historia de la sexualidad*, Siglo xxi, México.

———. 1978. *Microfísica del poder*, La Piqueta, Madrid.

———. 1979a. *Historia de la locura en la época clásica*, fce, México.

———. 1992. *El orden del discurso*, Tusquets, Argentina.

Foucault, Michel. 1994. *Dits et Écrits*, vol. iv, Gallimard, París.

———. 2002. *Las palabras y las cosas. Una arqueología de las ciencias humanas*, Siglo xxi, Argentina.

———. 2004. *El pensamiento del afuera*, Pre-Textos, Valencia.

———. 2008. *Security, Territory, Population: Lectures at the Collège de France 1977–1978*. Picador, New York.

Fromm, Erich. 1987. *Anatomía de la destructividad humana*, Siglo xxi, Madrid.

Fukuyama, Francis. 1992. *El fin de la historia y el último hombre*, Planeta, Madrid.

Galcerán Huguet, Montserrat. 2009. *Deseo (y) libertad. Una investigación sobre los presupuestos de la acción colectiva*, Traficantes de Sueños, Madrid.

García Canclini, Néstor. 2005. *Hybrid Cultures: Strategies for Entering and Leaving Modernity*. University of Minnesota Press, Minneapolis.

García meseguer, Álvaro. 1977. *Lenguaje y discriminación sexual*, Editorial Motesinos, España.

Geertz, Clifford. 1978. *La interpretación de las culturas*, Gedisa, Barcelona.

Glenny, Misha. 2008. *McMafia: A Journey Through the Global Criminal Underworld*. Random House, New York.

Guattari, Félix & Rolnik, Suely. 2008. *Molecular Revolution in Brazil*. Semiotext(e), Los Angeles.

Halberstam, Judith. 2008. *Masculinidad femenina*, Egales, Madrid.

Haraway, Donna J. 1995. *Ciencia, cyborgs y mujeres. La reinvención de la naturaleza*, Cátedra, Madrid.

———. 2004. *Testigo_Modesto@SegundoMilenio.HombreHembra ©Conoce_Oncoratón, Feminismo y tecnociencia*, Editorial uoc, Barcelona.

Harding, Sandra. 1996. *Ciencia y feminismo*, Ediciones Morata, Madrid.

Harvey, David. 1989. *The Condition of Postmodernity: An Enquiry into the Origins of Cultural Change*, Wiley-Blackwell, Hoboken.

———. 2000. *Spaces of Hope*, University of California Press, Oakland.

Helfrich, Silke (ed.) 2001. *Género, feminismo y masculinidad en América Latina*, Ed. Henrich Böll, El Salvador.

Heller, Ágnes & Feher Ferenc. 1994. *Biopolitics*. Avebury, Vienna.

Heritage, J. 1984. *Garfinkel and Etnomethodology*, Polity Press, Cambridge, Mass.

Hierro, Graciela. 2002. *De la domesticación a la educación de las mexicanas*, Editorial Torres Asociados, México.

Hobbes, Thomas. 2003. *Leviatán*, Losada, Buenos Aires.

hooks, bell, et al. 2004. *Obras inapropiables. Feminismos desde las fronteras*, Traficantes de Sueños, Madrid.

Horkheimer, Max & Adorno Theodor. 2001. *Dialéctica de la Ilustración*, Editorial Trotta, Madrid.

Jameson, Frederick. 1992. *Postmodernism, or, The Cultural Logic of Late Capitalism*. Duke University Press, Durham.

Jiménez G. María Lucero Guerrero, Olivia Tena Guerrero (coords.) 2007. *Reflexiones sobre masculinidades y empleo*. unam, Centro Regional de Investigaciones Multidisciplinarias, México.

Klein, Naomi. 2001. *No Logo. El poder de las marcas*, Paidós, Barcelona.

Krauze de Kolteniuk, Rosa. 1986. *Introducción a la investigación filosófica*. Universidad Autónoma de México, México.

Kristeva, Julia et al. 1985. *Travesía de los signos*, Ediciones la Auroirra, Argentina.

León G. Natalia Catalina. 2006, *Género, subjetividad y populismo: fantasmagorías de la política contemporánea*, Editorial Abya Yala, Ecuador.

Le Bras-Chopard, Armelle. 2003. *El zoo de los filósofos*, Taurus, Madrid.

Le Gallo, Yolande. 1988. *Nuevas máscaras, comedia antigua. Las representaciones de las mujeres en la televisión mexicana*. Premia Editora, México.

Liddell, Angélica. 2007. *Perro muerto en tintorería: los fuertes*, Centro Dramático Nacional, Madrid.

Lins Ribeiro, Gustavo. 2003. *Postimperialismo. Cultura y política en el mundo contemporáneo*, Gedisa, Barcelona.

Lipovetsky, Gilles. 2002. Trans. Catherine Porter. *The Empire of Fashion: Dressing Modern Democracy*, Princeton University Press, Princeton.

———. 2000b. *La tercera mujer*, Anagrama, Barcelona.

———. 2007. *La felicidad paradójica. Ensayo sobre la sociedad hiper-consumista*, Anagrama, Barcelona.

Lomas, Carlos (comp.) 2003 *¿Todos los hombres son iguales? Identidades masculinas y cambios sociales*, Paidós, Barcelona.

López Pardiña, Teresa Oliva Portolés Asunción (eds.) 2003. *Crítica feminista al psicoanálisis y a la filosofía*, Instituto de Investigaciones Feministas/ucm, Madrid.

Lyotard, Jean-François. 1989. *La condición posmoderna*. Cátedra, Barcelona.

——. 1992. *¿Por qué filosofar?*, Paidós, Barcelona.

Maldonado, Calos Eduardo. 2003. *Biopolítica de la guerra*, Siglo del Hombre Editores/ Universidad Libre/ Facultad de Filosofía, Colombia.

Mignolo, Walter. 2012. *Local Histories/Global Designs: Coloniality, Subaltern Knowledges, and Border Thinking*, Princeton University Press, Princeton.

Maquiavelo, Nicolás. 2004. *El príncipe*, Síntesis, Madrid.

Marx, Karl. 1992. *Capital*, Penguin, New York.

Mezzadra, Sandro. 2005. *Derecho de fuga. Migraciones, ciudadanía y globalización*, Traficantes de Sueños, Madrid.

Mezzadra, S., Chakravorty, S., Talpade, M., Shohat, E. et al. 2008. *Estudios Postcoloniales. Ensayos Fundamentales*, Traficantes de Sueños, Madrid.

Minh-Ha, Trinh T. 1989. *Women, Native, Other*, Indiana University Press, Bloomingston.

Montesinos, Rafael. 2007. *Perfiles de la masculinidad*, Universidad Autónoma Metropolitana/Plaza y Valdés, México.

Montezemolo, Fiamma, Peralta, René Yépez, Heriberto. 2006. *Here Is Tijuana*, Black Dog Publishing, London.

Moraga, Cherríe & Anzaldúa, Gloria. 1983. *This Bridge Called My Back: Writings by Radical Women of Color*. Kitchen Table/Women of Color Press, San Francisco.

Nietzsche, Friedrich 1997 (1886). *Más allá del bien y el mal*. Alianza editorial, Madrid.

——. 2006 (1887). *La genealogía de la moral*. Alianza Editorial, Madrid.

Negri, Antonio & Cocco Giussepe 2006. *Global. Biopoder y luchas en una América latina globalizada*, Paidós, Argentina.

Osborne, Richard & Edney Ralph 1996. *Filosofía. Desde la edad de la Razón al Posmodernismo*, Era Naciente, Buenos Aires.

Palaversich, Diana. 2005. *De Macondo a McOndo: senderos de la posmodernidad latinoamericana*, Plaza y Valdés, México.

Paz, Octavio. 1985. *Vuelta al laberinto de la soledad*, fce, México.

———. 1970. *Posdata*, fce, México.

———. 2002. *El laberinto de la soledad*, fce, México.

Pécaut, D. 2001. *Guerra contra la sociedad*, Espasa, Colombia.

Platón. 1985. *El Banquete, Diálogos*, Gredos, Madrid.

Pratt, Mary, Louise. 2002. *Globalization, Demodernization and the Return of the Monsters*, Third Encounter of Performance and Politics at the Universidad Católica, Lima, Peru.

Precarias a la Deriva. 2004. *A la deriva por los circuitos de la precariedad femenina*, Traficantes de Sueños, Madrid.

Preciado, Paul B. 2002. *Manifiesto contra-sexual. Prácticas subversivas de identidad sexual*, Opera Prima, Madrid.

———. 2013. *Testo Junkie: Sex, Drugs, and Biopolitics in the Pharmacopornographic Era*, The Feminist Press at CUNY, New York.

Puwar, Nirmal. 2004. *Space Invaders. Race, Gender And Bodies Out Of Place*, Berg, Nueva York.

Rangel, Leo & Moses-Hrushoski, Rena (eds.) 1996. *Psychoanalysis at the Political Border*, Madison.

Rivera Garretas, María-Milagros. 1994. *Nombrar el mundo en femenino. Pensamiento de las mujeres y teoría feminista*, Icaria, Barcelona.

Rodríguez de Montalvo Garci. 2006. *Amadís de Gaula*, Simancas Ediciones, Dueñas.

Sandoval Álvarez, Rafael. 2006. *Nuevas formas de hacer política. Una subjetividad emergente*, Universidad de Guadalajara, México.

Sáez, Javier. 2004. *Teoría Queer y psicoanálisis*, Síntesis, Madrid.

Santaemilia José, Gallardo, Beatriz i Sanmartín, Julia eds. 2002. *Sexe i llenguatge. La construcció lingüística de les identitats de génere*, Universitat de València, Valencia.

Saviano, Roberto. 2008. *Gomorrah: A Personal Journey into the Violent International Empire of Naples' Organized Crime System.* Farrar, Straus & Giroux, New York.

Schumpeter, Joseph. 1996. *Capitalismo, socialismo y democracia*, Folio, Barcelona.

Sennett, Richard. 2006. *La cultura del nuevo capitalismo*, Anagrama, Barcelona.

Shapin, Steven & Schaffer, Simon. 1985. *Leviathan and the Air-Pump: Hobbes, Boyle and the Experimental Life*, Princeton University Press, Princeton.

Sautu, Ruth. 2003. *Todo es Teoría. Objetivos y métodos de la investigación*, Ediciones Lumiere, Argentina.

Tijoux, María Emilia & Trujillo, Iván (comps.) 2006. *Foucault fuera de sí. Deseo, Historia, Subjetividad*, Editorial arcis, Santiago de Chile.

Tilly, Charles. 2003. *The Politics of Collective Violence*, Cambridge Univerisity Press, New York.

Ugarte pérez, Javier (comp.) 2005. *La administración de la vida. Estudios biopolíticos*, Anthropos, Barcelona.

Valencia, Triana, M. (comp.) 2009. *Latin Queer*, Centaurea Nigra Ediciones, Madrid.

Vallejo, Fernando. 1997. *Logoi. Una gramática del lenguaje literario*, fce, México.

Varela, Nuria. 2005. *Feminismo para principiantes*, Ediciones B, Barcelona.

Vidarte, Francisco. 2007. *Ética marica*, Egales, Madrid.

Villaplana, Virginia. 2008. *Zona de intensidades*, Aconcagua Publishing, Madrid.

Villaplana, Virginia & Sichel, Berta. 2005. *Cárcel de Amor. Relatos culturales sobre la violencia de género*, Museo Nacional Centro de Arte Reina Sofía, Madrid.

Virilio, Paul. 2003. *Estética de la desaparición*, Anagrama, Barcelona.

Virno, Paolo. 2003. *Gramática de la multitud*, Traficantes de Sueños, Madrid.

Watts, Barry. 1984. *The Foundations of US Air Doctrine*, Maxwell Air Force Base.

Wittgenstein, Ludwig. 1999. *Tractatus Logico-Philosophicus*, Alianza, Madrid.

Witting, Monique. 2006. *El pensamiento heterosexual y otros ensayos*, Egales, Madrid.

Ziga, Itziar. 2009. *Devenir perra*, Melusina, Barcelona.

Žižek, Slavoj. 2002. *Welcome to the Desert of the Real*, Verso, New York.

Articles

Agamben, Giorgio. "I am sure that you are more pessimistic than I am…": An interview with Giorgio Agamben by Jason Smith. *Rethinking Marxism*, Vol. 16 , Iss. 2, 2004

Alcoff, Linda. Primavera de 2000. "Philosophy matters; a review of recent work in feminist philosophy," *Signs*, vol. 25, no 3.

Alzaga, Ignacio.(24/01/2009). "Capturan a El Pozolero; cocinó a 300 narcos: Sedena," *Milenio*, México, D. F.

Anónimo, "Reclutan Zetas a militares en Guatemala con Spot de radio." *El informador*. Diario Independiente. 24/04/2008. Guadalajara, México. http://www.eluniversal.com.mx/notas/501252.html

Aznárez, Juan. 23/11/2008. "Quiero Ser Pirata," *El País*, Madrid.

Bares, Mauricio. 23/05/2008. "Violencia Ancestral," *Reforma*, suplemento cultural, México, D. F.

Belin, Henri & Arbizu, Susana. 07/02/2008. "Teoría king kong" [entrevista a Virginie Despentes], *Eutsi.org*.

Cruz, Juan. 18/04/2008. "El primer mandamiento es no dañar" [entrevista a Adela Cortina], *El País Semanal*, Madrid.

Espinosa, Guillermo. 20/04/2008. "Siniestra Belleza," *El País semanal*, Madrid.

Finas, L. Enero de 1977. "Las relaciones de poder penetran en los cuerpos" [entrevista a Michel Foucault], *La Quinzaine Littéraire*, no 247, pp. 1–15, París.

Grelet, Stany & Potte-Bonneville, Mathieu. Invierno 1999–2000. "Una biopolítica menor" [entrevista a Giorgio Agamben], *Vacarme*, no 10, París.

Guerra Palmero, María José. 2001. "Arrojando el guante: la construcción social de la masculinidad," *Teoría feminista contemporánea. Una aproximación desde la ética*. Instituto de Investigaciones Feministas/ Universidad Complutense de Madrid, Madrid.

Gutiérrez R. Encarnación. 2006. "Traduciendo Posiciones. Sobre coyunturas postcoloniales y entendimiento transversal," *Translate. Beyond Culture: The Politics of Translation*.

Foucault, Michel. 1979b. "Nacimiento de la biopolítica," revista *Archipiélago*, no 30, pp. 119–124.

Galcerán Huguet, Montserrat. Mayo-junio de 2008. "Autonomía y subjetividad. Por una lectura crítica de algunos textos de A. Negri," www.youkali.net, no 5.

Goenaga, Gorka. 23/07/2008. "La identidad no existe" [entrevista a Orlan], revista *Shangay Express*, no 336. Año xiv, Madrid.

Lavigne, Chris. 1/29/2005. "Bloody Well Done," http://www.game-brains.com/archive/jan17_2005/gta_sanandreas.htm

Lazzarato, Maurizio. March 2000. "From Biopower to Biopolitics," *The Warwick Journal of Philosophy*, London.

Mbembe, Achille. Marzo de 1999. "Du Gouvernement privé indirect," *Politique Africaine*, no 73, pp. 103–121, París.

——. 2003. "Necropolitics," *Public Culture*, vol. 15, no 1, pp. 11–40, Duke University Press, Durham.

Mignolo, Walter. 2003b. "Las geopolíticas del conocimiento y la colonialidad del poder, *Polis*, Universidad Bolivariana de Chile, vol. 1, no 4.

Monsiváis, Carlos. Abril-mayo, 1981. "¿Pero hubo alguna vez once mil machos?," *FEM*, no 18, pp. 9–20, México.

Mora, Miguel. 20/04/2008. "El hombre que novela la corrupción" [entrevista a Massimo Carlotto], *El País Semanal*, Madrid.

Moulier-Boutang. Yan. Marzo de 2000. "Eclats d´economie et bruit de lutes," *Multitudes*, no 2, París.

Negri, Antonio & Cocco, Giuseppe. 10/07/2007. "La insurrección de las periferias," *Caosmosis*, http://caosmosis.acracia.net

Noam Warner, Daniel. Primer trimestre de 2005. "Hacia una metodología de la investigación *queer*," *Orientaciones. Revista de homosexualidades*, no 9.

Ordaz, Pablo. 23/11/2008. "El crimen organizado estaba tocando a las puertas del Estado" [entrevista a Eduardo Medina Mora], *El País*, Madrid.

——. 14/06/2009. "Cuando mata La Familia" en www.elpais.com.

Pla, Erkhiñe. 15/05/2008. "Una entrevista con Chantal Maillard," *Diario de Noticias de Navarra*, Huarte-Pamplona.

Preciado, Beatriz. 2009a. "Transfeminismos y micropolíticas del género en la era farmacopornográfica," *Artecontexto*, no 21, Madrid.

——. 2009b. "Historia de una palabra: *queer*," *Parole de queer*, no 1, Barcelona.

Saavedra, Rafael. 13/12/2008. "Sobreviviendo Tijuana," *Milenio*, suplemento Laberinto, México, D. F.

Sassen, Saskia. 2000. "Women's Burden: Counter-geographies of Globalization and the Feminization of Survival." *Journal of International Affairs*, 53, 2.

Sloterdijk, Peter. 2009. "Rules for the Human Zoo." *Environment and Planning*, vol. 27 (2009), pgs 12–28.

Subcomandante Marcos. August 1997. "The Fourth World War Has Begun." *Nepantla: Views from the South*. 2:3.

Resa Nestares, Carlos (1997). "Delincuencia y desempleo: la historia de una relación contradictoria." *Sistema. Revista de Ciencias Sociales*, vols. 140–41 (1997), págs. 265–84.

——. "La organización de la producción de drogas en México." (Nota de investigación, 27 de febrero de 2001). http://www.uam.es/personal_pdi/economicas/cresa//text10.html

——. "Las drogas en el México post-Arellano Félix." (Nota de investigación 03/2002), http://www.uam.es/personal_pdi/economicas/cresa//nota0302.pdf

——. "El ejército mexicano y el comercio ilegal de drogas." (Nota de investigación 04/2002), http://www.uam.es/personal_pdi/economicas/cresa//nota0402.pdf

——. "La *nueva* policía mexicana." (Nota de investigación 01/2003). http://www.uam.es/personal_pdi/economicas/cresa//nota0103.pdf

——. "El comercio de drogas y los conceptos míticos: la plaza." (Nota de investigación 02/2003), http://www.uam.es/personal_pdi/economicas/cresa//nota0203.pdf

——. "La prensa, los "cárteles" y el comercio de drogas en 2003."(Nota de investigación 03/2003) http://www.uam.es/personal_pdi/economicas/cresa//nota0403.pdf

——. "Los Zetas: de narcos a mafiosos." (Notas de investigación 04/ 2003), http://www.uam.es/personal_pdi/economicas/cresa//nota0403.pdf

——. "El comercio de drogas ilegales en México. Corrupción en la pgr: promesas sin seguimiento."(Nota de investigación 05/2003), http://www.uam.es/personal_pdi/economicas/cresa//nota0503.pdf

———. "El valor de las exportaciones mexicanas de drogas ilegales, 1961–2000." Universidad Autónoma de Madrid, 2003. http://www.uam.es/ personal_pdi/economicas/cresa//uam2003.pdf

———. "El crimen organizado transnacional: definición, causas y consecuencias" [Transnational Organized Crime: Definition, Causes and Consequences]. http://www.uam.es/personal_pdi/economicas/cresa//text11.html

———. "La mafia rusa y el espíritu del capitalismo" [The Russian Mafia and the Spirit of Capitalism]. http://www.taringa.net/posts/info/1258047/La-mafia-rusa-y-el-esp%C3%ADritu-del-capitalismo.html

———. "Macroeconomía de las drogas" [Macroeconomics of Drugs]. peyote inc, http://www.geocities.com/carlos_resa/press18.html

———. "El crimen organizado transnacional: definición, causas y consecuencias" [Transnational Organized Crime: Definition, Causes and Consequences]. http://www.uam.es/personal_pdi/economicas/cresa//text11.html

———. "El Dinero adicto a las drogas" [Money Addicted to Drugs]. peyote inc. http://www.geocities.com/carlos_resa/press14.html

Ruesga, Santos / Resa, Carlos. 02/09/1997. "Mafiosos, estraperlistas y piratas," *El Mundo*, año ix, no 2845.

Yépez, Heriberto. 29/01/2008. "Receta para cocinar narco a la parrilla," *Milenio*. Suplemento Laberinto, México, D. F.

Others

Butler, Judith. 26/05/2008. "Critique, Dissent, and Violence," Seminar at cendeac, Murcia.

———. 08/06/2009. "Performativity, Precarity and Sexual Politics." Conferencia impartida en la Facultad de Ciencias de la Información, ucm, Madrid.

Liddell, Angélica. 23/05/2008. *3ra. desobediencia. Yo no soy bonita ni lo quiero ser*, La Casa Encendida, Madrid.

Lozoya, José Ángel. Mayo de 2002. "Hombres por la igualdad."(Delegación de Salud y género) en las Jornadas de Género y Sexualidad. La Laguna.

Lunch, Lydia. 2004. *Vendo frustración, no alivio. Real Pornography*. Music Performance.

Medem, Julio. 2003. *La Pelota Vasca*. Género: documental, duración 115 min., España.

Manifiesto: *con fronteras no hay orgullo*. Lesbianas, Gays, Trans, Bisex, Queer y Heteros contra la ley de extranjería y la represión a l@s inmigrantes. Madrid, 27 de junio de 2009.

Ritchie, Guy. 2008. *Rockanrolla*. Género: acción, duración: 114 min., Reino Unido.

Sisteaga, Jon. 26 de diciembre 2008 & 02 enero de 2009. *NarcoMéxico: alfombra roja para los muertos*. Género: Información/ Investigación. Episodios 1 & 2, TV-4, España.